THE ELEVENTH COMMANDMENT

THE ELEVENTH COMMANDMENT

MENNONITE LOW GERMAN SHORT STORIES BY
JACK THIESSEN

RE-WORKED AND TRANSLATED BY
ANDREAS SCHROEDER

Thistledown Press

Canadian Cataloguing in Publication Data
Schroeder, Andreas, 1946-
  The eleventh commandment
  ISBN 0-920633-80-3

I. Thiessen, Jack, 1931-   II. Title

PS8587.C5E43 1990 839'.43 C90-097148-7
PR9199.3.S34E43 1990

Book design by A.M. Forrie
Cover etching by K. Gwen Frank

Typeset by Thistledown Press Ltd.

Thistledown Press Ltd.
668 East Place
Saskatoon, Saskatchewan
S7J 2Z5

Acknowledgements

This book has been published with the assistance of
The Canada Council and the Saskatchewan Arts Board

CONTENTS

INTRODUCTION

The Eleventh Commandment is a collection of Jack Thiessen's oral Low-German Mennonite stories and tales that have been published serially in Canada over about a decade. I have been gathering, reworking and translating them for book publication since the early 1980's. Since they stem from an oral tradition, however, I have tried to retain as many of their oral elements and characteristics as possible.

To put these stories into context, a brief history of the Mennonites may be helpful. A radical Anabaptist sect dating from approximately 1525, the Mennonites grew into two fairly distinct movements — one largely Swiss-German in origin, the other North German/Dutch. The North German/Dutch group eventually settled in the Lower Vistula region near the present-day city of Gdansk (Poland), and it was here that their traditional Low German *(Plattdeutsch)* became established. (The Swiss-German Mennonites, many of whom moved to the U.S. in response to an invitation from William Penn in 1683, also established a Germanic dialect, Pennsylvania German, commonly misnomered "Pennsylvania Dutch". The two dialects, however, are quite different.)

The North German/Dutch Mennonite group eventually accepted an invitation by Russia's Catherine the Great in 1788 and colonized large parts of the present-day Ukraine. For the next century, Mennonite life and culture flourished as never before, and it was during this time that the main body of Mennonite Low German literature was built up. However, Mennonite religious leaders were generally suspicious of "secular literature", and only a few significant Low-German authors developed a substantial body of work (*i.e.*, Arnold Dyck, Fritz Senn).

Between 1874 and 1930, several large immigration waves brought Mennonites of North German/Dutch ancestry from the Ukraine to both Canada and the United States. Here they linked up to some extent with the Swiss-German Mennonites of earlier immigrations, but maintained largely separate churches and cultures. Thus the term "Mennonite" implies significantly different cultural origins, depending on who is using the term. The Mennonite Low-German stories of Jack Thiessen were all engendered in Canada, though some are set in the Ukraine. All reflect Thiessen's North German/Dutch affiliation and ancestry.

Low German among the Mennonites was used primarily for "domestic" consumption — which is to say, in the home. In church, Mennonites generally spoke High German. Thus Low German has been until relatively recently entirely oral — *i.e.*, it has had no formal rules of spelling or grammar. (There are now several groups of Mennonite scholars who have begun to agree on certain rules and have produced listings of standardized spellings, but these have not yet been widely accepted.)

Perhaps 250,000 Mennonites in Canada, the U.S.A., Mexico and South America still speak (or can understand) Low German. But the disintegration of this dialect is proceeding with breath-taking speed. The passage of a single generation will cut that number down to fewer than 50,000. Ironically, while the total world Mennonite population is growing vigorously, its wonderfully cheeky and irreverent "domestic languages" are fast fading away.

Andreas Schroeder
Mission, B.C.

AUNT MARGARET'S DEMISE

(Tante Jreeta Stoawt)

When we heard that Great-Aunt Margaret was coming over from Russia, after the Second World War, we envisioned her as a little heap of misfortune we might be carrying — who knew — to her grave within the year. "Yes, she'll be old and frail by now," said Aunt Anna. "She's bound to have lost her appetite. After what she went through during the war, poor thing, I wouldn't be the least surprised. She's probably already lost her will to live."

That September in 1949 we got dressed in our Sunday best and all drove down to the C.P.R. station in Winnipeg to pick her up. All the way from Gruenthal to Winnipeg, father and mother speculated about how she would look. They both agreed she'd barely be able to walk, that she'd eat less than a sparrow. How sad, how very very sad. She had always been such a substantial woman, one hundred and eighty pounds and no fat at all; to have to see her now, all withered, her face wrinkled as frog's leather, not to mention her hands. It was a terrible shame.

We had only just reached the station and were about to ask whether the train was on time or what, when a woman charged out from behind a stone pillar, grabbed me in a wrestler's clutch and began hugging and kissing the dickens out of me. It was Aunt Margaret! She had seen us, had hidden behind a pillar, and had prepared an ambush. The train had come in earlier that day.

"But how did you know who I was? You've never seen me before," I wanted to know.

"Your nose, my boy, your unmistakable nose! You have the Thiessen trunk!"

I stood back a little and sized up my "frail old aunt". "I'm not so sure about us, but *she'll* certainly last the night," I decided.

Meanwhile Aunt Margaret wasn't taking any chances. As soon as we'd arrived home she sat us down and pinned us with a stern look. "Now listen, all of you: I may have only a few hours left in this world, and I want to reassure myself. Are you all properly prepared for His Coming, or don't you belong to the Mennonite Brethren Church yet?" I hurried out to the barn to do chores.

When I returned Aunt Margaret was sitting at the table, and if I'd had any doubts before about our being closely related, those doubts immediately evaporated. The huge plate before her was heaped with no less than a full ring of smoked farmer's sausage, a mound of headcheese, at least five cubic inches of collared pork, and a whole cupful of vinegar.

And then she started to talk — and Lord God in heaven, this aunt was some talker. She told us all about the Whites and the Reds, the Russians and the Blacks, of relatives and half-believers, of heretics and the Molotschna. She talked so animatedly and so rousingly, I kept finding myself forgetting to breathe; when she described how she'd let one particularly bad Russian have it with a fork handle and then demonstrated the blow with a powerful sweep of her arm, she knocked me clean off my chair.

For the first time in our lives we went to bed after twelve o'clock that night, Aunt Margaret still talking furiously, because after all, there was always the chance it might be her last night in this vale of tears. "But if it isn't, Lena, then please cook me some borscht tomorrow, and roast a good goose, and maybe a fat rooster, and don't forget the stuffing! Oh and Peter — could you see your way clear to bringing in a sealer of *kwas* from the granary?" Having thus assured herself of the next day's provisions, she headed for the corner cupboard and attacked a bottle of *Alpenkraeuter* with such enthusiasm, the sight of her vigorously bobbing Adam's apple remains vividly in my memory to this day. Then we finally all went to bed.

Next day was Sunday. When I got in from the barn Aunt Margaret was already in the midst of another tale. Yes yes, she had slept quite well, she had had a bit of discomfort what with her spleen acting up again, probably from all the excitement — but other than that she felt just fine. "Oh yes, if back in Russia we'd had a little lunch like the one we had last night, they wouldn't have had the Communism over there, I guarantee you that. But you can't cook a decent soup from broomweed, and if you don't give the Russian boys a good solid wallop every morning they're snooty again by the afternoon."

"Listen Hans," she said to me then. "Do I look to you as if I'm going to die very soon?"

"No," I said with some conviction. "You're not yellow around the eyes yet. And besides," I said, "your appetite is still pretty good."

"You mean that little snack we had last night?"

"Uh-huh," I said.

"Ach so," she said.

After church we sat down at the table; the house had filled with relatives and visitors. Aunt Margaret hadn't seen any of these people in twenty-five years but she looked at their noses, compared their gestures, listened to their voices and then delivered her verdicts: "You're George's second child!" and "You must be Sarah's cousin!" or "You would be Peter Dyck's daughter; wasn't your father the disgraced minister?" To Connie Hiebert she said: "Ah yes, you are Mrs. Hiebert's autumn chicken, the late child. We thought your mother would have a miscarriage and there was all sorts of talk of doctoring around with you, but now look at you — a good solid woman. . . yes yes. . . but tell me, what is it with you people in this country, you seem to have become a little thick-skinned; I didn't see a soul crying in church this morning!"

Did I forget to mention that during all this she was munching and swallowing as if there might be no tomorrow? Oh yes: four bowls of borscht that evaporated like water under an August sun; a pile of rooster legs and half a goose which reappeared in short order as a neat pile of gleaming bones; slice after slice of cooked ham, and from the heap of plum pits you could see that at least half a tureen of fruit soup had found its final resting place in the depths of Aunt Margaret. But all the while she kept talking, exhorting, proselytizing; people laughed and they cried and they exlaimed: "What a world, what a world!" Some were so moved, they even opened their billfolds.

Aunt Margaret soon left for British Columbia — the ground wasn't as hard there in the winter; you could die there anytime you wanted — leaving us sitting in Gruenthal, set to go to B.C. at a moment's notice. "Because I could die any day now," she assured us. "Oh yes, it could happen any day now. Anyone who can cross the ocean can also die." And she heaped up her plate.

✦ ✦ ✦

Thirteen years later I visited her in B.C. And again I sat by her side as she ate, and she told me stories. And then she leaned over to me confidentially and said: "Listen Hans, will you promise me that when I've spooned out my last little dish, you'll come to my funeral? You will? That's good. And now tell me, Hans, you are so educated now, give me your opinion. Do you think a dead person can. . . well, you know. . . attend her own funeral?"

"Probably," I hazarded.

"Well, that's exactly the way I see it too! And because of that, I need new material for a dress!"

We immediately climbed into my car and drove off to a wholesaler to buy cotton and silk for a black jumper and a white blouse. As soon as we got back Aunt Margaret phoned for a seamstress, who arrived half an hour later with scissors and needles. There was a great deal of measuring and cutting and fussing, and then the old Singer began to hum its age-old tune. And while all this was going on I was sent out to buy strawberries, raspberries and a watermelon; just the contemplation of her long last voyage had made Aunt Margaret very hungry.

When we had finished eating and her funeral clothes were ready — white on top, black beneath — she sat down in her new wardrobe, folded her hands and cried a little. "I'm a bit afraid, now that I'm ready; when you're 81 years old, that final knock at your little door can come at any moment. Will you stay with me until tomorrow? Actually, I'd always thought I might get married in Canada, but I don't suppose anything will come of it. What do you think, Hans?"

"Well, I'll tell you," I said, "I know of a perky old bachelor in Germany who's available, old Adenauer you know, if that's any help. . . "

"Stop those rude remarks," she admonished sternly. "You know perfectly well he's a Catholic."

"I'm sorry," I apologized.

The next morning, at breakfast, Aunt Margaret ate so heartily that her pension cheque crumbled with every bite. No, she wasn't gone yet, she informed me, though she had her ticket in her pocket. But while I'd tossed on the livingroom sofa she'd been dreaming she'd gone to heaven, and it had been so wonderful, she told me, she was finding things on earth a little flat this morning.

✦   ✦   ✦

It wasn't until the spring of 1967, when she was 93, that Aunt Margaret finally gave in to heaven's blandishments. She had just finished a little lunch — cooked ham, noodles, onions and cold fruit soup — when a bit of pain here, a little pinch there, convinced her to "lay her ear on her mattress" for a few minutes. This time she didn't rise again. And when it was all over, we opened the window and set her spirit free.

Aunt Margaret had worn out four jumpers and five blouses practising for her funeral. Now she lay in her coffin and smiled a bit. In the middle of the sermon I turned around and had another good look at her. Yes, I believe to this day she was enjoying herself. And she didn't look the least bit hungry.

KLASSEN'S MELON PATCH

(Bie Klossess Enne Berstaund)

In 1936 it was so horribly hot and so dreadfully dry, that many people thought the Day of Judgement had finally come. In the barn the chicks gaped open-beaked for air and water, and the ducks rejoiced if you so much as spat at them. The frogs in the ditches all sang bass, and at the Peter Schellenberg farm they were so short of water, the cows gave butter dumplings instead of milk. Even the churches had to make adjustments; it was so dry that the Mennonite Brethren started baptising with a water-jug, while the General Conference issued rain checks.

And in Winnipeg it was even worse. Returning Gruenthalers reported that cars were bogging down in the boiling asphalt, and people were frying eggs on the sidewalks rather than heat up their stoves. In the Assiniboine Park Zoo the monkeys had taken to singing the Sons of the Pioneers' "Cool, clear water" in two-part harmony at dusk.

"Yes folks, it's hot," said Pankratz as he scratched at the diminishing thatch on his head. Then he went inside. The children had begun to wear shoes again, the sand and stones in the yard were so hot — as hot as the Fiery Ovens they had learned about in Sunday school. Long-Legged Hiebert moaned and said, "May the Devil inherit this manurepile of a creation!" — though he waited until his wife had gone inside before he said it —

and then he said he might just as well have stayed in Russia.

"But there are two sides to everything," old Eva Klassen reminded everybody. "And this year we'll have a dandy watermelon crop."

Well, that's exactly what happened. There were so many watermelons that year that Rempel finally sold them at three dollars a wagonload. Everybody preserved watermelon syrup by the ton; Mrs. Unger baked watermelon cobbler just like in Russia. People undressed their children and let them eat their fill at the watermelon patch twice a day. They stored cut-up watermelon in crocks; they dried the seeds and salted them down with rock salt. All of southern Manitoba smelled of fritters — the mandatory culinary accompaniment to watermelons.

Now a Russian family, the Tilitzkys, who lived close to the Klassens, hadn't gotten around to starting their garden until June, and whatever the cutworms hadn't gotten had fallen prey to the pocket gophers. So they took to helping themselves to Klassen's melons at night, sneaking into his patch and thumping them to find the ripest ones. These they smashed with their fists and then ate them on the spot, seeds and all.

Klassen looked up Tilitzky. "Your boys seem to get lost at night and end up in my melon patch. Now you keep them on your side of the fence, or I might be tempted to warm their backsides according to an old and proven recipe."

Tilitzky reddened. "To hell with you! My boys sleep at night. It's the German snotnoses who're pilfering your miserable melons. So don't get me mad." And he went back inside.

Klassen hollered after him: "So if I happen to hit anyone in the ass with my twelve-gauge, it won't be one of your boys?"

"Damn right," Tilitzky hollered back.

Klassen went back to his place and rolled himself an Old Chum. Then he helped himself to a particularly large and juicy watermelon. That night he stayed at home, but the next evening he took out a shotgun shell, emptied it, and poured in some rocksalt instead. He shoved this shell into his twelve-gauge, and when it was dark, lay down in his melon patch to wait.

The moon rose in all its splendour, the crickets chirped, the coyotes howled lazily, a sheep bleated. Everyone was asleep, and all of nature was replenishing itself. Only Klassen lay wide awake on the warm earth of his melon patch. He thought about his relatives scattered all over the globe; he thought about the beautiful farm he'd had to abandon in Russia; he thought about the confounded stones in his sheep pasture. Then he rolled himself another Old Chum and waited some more among the vines. The moon, gazing at the earth as nosily as a peeping Tom, noticed that people here and there were being rather naughty, and so it looked with particular approval on Klassen and his gun among the watermelon leaves.

"Just wait and see," Klassen thought to himself. "You smart-ass pumpkin in the sky." But he was pleased that the moon smiled on him so nicely. Suddenly he heard a noise, and he doused his Old Chum. And sure enough, there came the Tilitsky rascals. "One could almost believe one was back in Russia on the Dnieper," Klassen thought. "The air, the earth, the watermelons, the moon, and now these Ukrainians."

Tilitsky's Peter bent down, thumped a melon, tore it off its vine and ate, once, twice, three times. "Well that's okay," Klassen calculated. "Let him have a few; we've got enough." But the greedy lad had brought a sack, a bag and a cardboard box, and now he began to fill them up. "*Bozhe, pomozhe,*" said Klassen to himself. "This is too much for any true-blooded farmer. . ." And he thought briefly of a heroic line or two of Teutonic poetry, closed one eye, and gently lifted the shotgun just as the lad bent down and thumped another melon. In his sights Klassen saw a black double moon. The barrel froze. "*Pasholl!*" Klassen hollered, and pulled the trigger. Tilitsky's Peter yelped "*Tschorrt!*", leaped clean to the fence — the next day Klassen determined the distance to be thirty-four feet — and cleared its eight feet in a single bound. "*Postoj!*" Klassen hollered after him, but the lad was too busy setting Olympic records for the broad-jump, the high-jump and the hundred-yard dash. Klassen ambled home, rolled himself an Old Chum, and just grinned when his wife mentioned that she'd heard the Tilitzky barn door bang rather loudly that morning. "Think I'll go over to the Tilitskys for a game of checkers," he told her after breakfast.

And that's what he did. He won three games in handy succession. "Tell me, Pietro Wailowitch, where's your eldest?" he asked casually as he stacked up the checkers.

"No idea," Tilitsky shrugged.

"We should find him; I'll offer him a game," Klassen said. "Let's go look for him."

They found young Peter in the barn with his pants pulled down, and his rear submerged in a tub of warm water. He didn't even try to get up — just sat there meekly as a limp frog. There were watermelon seeds in his hair, and watermelon seeds on his shoes. He looked sheepish and said that from now on he was prepared to believe in the Devil more fervently. "What happened?" Klassen wanted to know.

"He has poison ivy," Tilitsky replied.

"Our remedy for that is salt," Klassen advised. "Just rub salt on it, and it'll go away."

"And incidentally," he added. "I found a sack, a bag and a cardboard box in my melon patch this morning. Do you have any use for them?" And as he turned away, chuckling to himself, he rolled himself a final Old Chum.

FIRST PRIZE

(Easchta Pries)

Yes, it was a day of surprises. Just as we were smelling the sweet aroma of workday's end, somebody called: "Come quickly, have a look at this, oh, this is the most hilarious..." and we all dropped whatever we were doing that late August day and rushed over to have a look, and someone said, "Can you believe that?" and father said, "Almost as good as in Russia", and mother said, "Not even ashamed, and in bright daylight too." There, in the yard, were Redbright, Longlegs and Bossy, our three cows, all hot and uncomfortable, their great udders so full, their teats were streaming milk. And underneath, catching this milkshower with muzzles agape, a writhing frenzy of milk froth-covered piglets sucked and smacked and squealed joyously. It was a sight to behold.

We had barely watched our fill of this charming scene when the put-put-puttering of an automobile engine reached our ears, and to our utter astonishment, the shiny new car that bounced and jolted into the yard from behind the summer kitchen contained our hugely pleased-looking neighbour, Sabbather Koop. As he brought the car to a shuddering stop, he pressed its horn, "Uh Ah, Uh Ah!", jumped out and took up position against one gleaming mudguard, placing his hands under his overall suspenders and clasping them tightly over his chest. From this perspective he could see the entire Thiessen bunch at a glance, and feed like one of our piglets on our satisfying amazement and envy.

For the first time since we'd come to Canada my father was too startled to say anything immediately. Once he'd gradually come to, he shrugged. "Take a good look at this mister, children; he's a true *kulak.*" My mother, on the other hand, just stood there, gazing silently, and her eyes suddenly reminded me of a photo album; in them I could see pictures of Russia, and a big prosperous estate and a happy, ordered life... And though I would never have told her this, and she would have called it nonsense if I had, I could also see her thoughts, which read: "It is I who belong in that car", but aloud she said: "Well well, Mistah Koop, from now on we should probably call you Elias, don't you think?" But Koop stood there happily, said nothing and smiled a lot, about his car, about us, and about both.

When Koop's intuition told him he had had the maximum benefit from our bug-eyed gazing, he said: "I have brought something along for you too. See?" and he pulled out two green-striped watermelons from underneath the backseat's cover, and then four yellow melons too. Right on cue, our jaws dropped again. For one thing, we'd never seen watermelons that big before, and secondly, because our mouths watered so excitedly, we were simply unable to speak.

"Now who would have figured that?" my father asked, but since he asked that question four or five times a day, it went unanswered. But the answer was: no one would have figured it, because none of us had ever seen Sabbather Koop's garden; we didn't visit with the Koops. You see, the Koops were Mennonites of a sort, but only barely, by the skin of their teeth. The best you could say about them was that they did speak an acceptable Low German. But then on Saturdays, when we were still sweating out the last day of the week in our fields, the Koops took the day off and praised the Lord, and on Sundays, when we had our enforced Day of Rest, Koop started up his tractor and rattled around all day in his fields.

So we had very little to do with the Koops. All we knew was that Koop had sandy soil and an artesian well that just wouldn't quit, so he always had more water than the rest of us. Nothing much else. In fact, I was rather surprised that the Good Lord would stoop to allowing them to grow such large melons. It didn't seem quite fair.

But if we'd had visions of hurling ourselves at these luscious melons to devour them gulp by gulp, we were in for our next surprise. As soon as Koop had driven off, father ordered us to fill a small wagon with straw, hoisted the melons gently into it and transported them to the ice cellar. And there in the shade he buried them in sawdust and ice, because the following Saturday was Exhibition Day in Gruenthal, and my father had something up his sleeve.

When Saturday arrived, we hitched our horses to a straw-filled wagon, bundled the melons into it, and headed off.

Oh boy oh boy oh boy did they ever have a spread at the Gruenthal Exhibition! Chicken coops on top of more chicken coops, and on top of that, on grey blankets, cream, cottage cheese and eggs, pies, ears of corn, proud deep-red tomatoes with water droplets still pearling down their sides, fat onions, carrots with their greens intact, countless sealers full of cocky cherries, cheeky crab-apples and dill pickles cozily snuggled up against each other.

Now, it was no secret that our Uncle Bill Thiessen had pretty well cleaned up on all the first and second prizes over the past years. This year again it was clear he had every intention of keeping his record perfect. He buzzed around all over the place, always knowing exactly what he wanted, dispensing advice in all directions, his energetic little feet spelling out the unmistakable message: "no surprises, no surprises, first prize, first prize" as he scurried along.

Father placed "our" melons a little to the back of the stands, in our cleaned and polished wheelbarrow full of hay and alfalfa with the purple blossoms still on. He laid the largest watermelon on its back with its fat pale belly facing upward, and the other beside it at a fetching angle, aimed right at the spectators. After at least a hundred people had had a look and commented, "Holy doodle, such watermelons! How on earth did you manage that, Thiessen?" and father had shrugged for the hundredth time and allowed as how he'd brought the seeds from the old country, the three judges approached. "Tell you what, my boy," father said to me, "your English is better than mine. You talk with these dressed-up gentlemen." Then he cut into the second watermelon with a large knife, placed four generous pieces onto one of mother's best china plates, and was gone.

The judges impressed me no end. Here it was only Saturday but they were dressed in their Sunday Best.

They were astonished at the watermelons and asked me where on earth one could grow such magnificent specimens here on the prairies. "Over by the Sabbathers, across the crick," I told them honestly.

"Such a modest little fellow, and good manners too," one of the judges smiled. And then they taste-tested the cut-up pieces until they were all gone, pinned "First Prize" on the fat-bellied one, "Second Prize" on the sampler, and then three more First, Second and Third prizes on the others. I just sat there open-mouthed, amazed at all the things this big world has in store for its children.

After two more hours or so, people started to disperse, and when most of them were gone, father returned. He pulled me behind the stands and showed me the eleven dollars he had won for the First Prize. Eleven dollars, all in one pile! My six-year-old eyes had never seen so much money. And then father said: "Wait here a bit," and when he returned he had a five-cent ice-cream cone in his hand, which I was allowed to eat all by myself.

UNCLE FALK'S HOT CANDY

(Onkel Faultj Siene Candy)

You've probably all heard that the summer of '36 was abominably hot and dry, but what you probably haven't heard is that the spring of '37 was extremely wet, and that as a six-year-old I had to help fix fences in water and mud up to my eyeballs. Yes, that's how it was. The mosquitoes were humming in all gears, whining and pricking me by the thousands, and even looking for blood in my clothes — you probably haven't heard that either. But that's what they did. And whenever I tried to wipe the sweat off my brow while fixing fences, my sleeve came away covered with blood.

But our cows, the stupid beasts, kept insisting on sampling the neighbour's oats, so we had to build a new fence. Heat, rain or mosquitoes, it didn't matter; we had to load up the schooner wagon with fence posts, barbed wire, a goose-neck, hammer, staples, pliers, a stretcher and a sledge-hammer. Then we threw on a syrup pail full of cold water, hitched up the horses, and off we went.

My brother Peter was eight and I had just turned seven and father had important things to do, very important things he said, so he sent along Uncle Cornelius Falk to do the job. Now Uncle Falk was an unusual man — a bit slow but tremendously powerful, weighed over three hundred pounds in the winter right after hog-butchering, and could stook sweet clover in his bare feet.

(Whether he was all that tough or whether he simply didn't own any shoes, I don't know; probably both.) A man like that didn't turn up every day, not even in Gruenthal. And he was very pious, never swore and didn't talk nonsense, people said. "Yessiree," my brother told me, "such a Mennonite Brethren uncle couldn't even get mad!"

So Uncle Falk was sent fencing with us. It was the beginning of July, ferociously hot and wet, wet and hot as hell, father said; too hot and too wet. When we arrived at the swamp, Peter had to hold the horses while Uncle Falk grabbed a fence post, sighted it into place, forced it a few inches into the ground, climbed back up onto the wagon, panting and groaning, and then said: "Hold onto that post, Hans. Now you just steady that post!" Bracing himself with one foot on the wagon and hooking the giant toes of his other onto the wagon box, he tapped the post experimentally with the sledge. "Hold it tight now!" he yelled, and then he wound up and swung, the mighty sledge-hammer crashing down onto the post, while mud and water sprayed all around. "Count!" he commanded. At the count of ten the post was rammed in tight and I was so covered with slime I could hardly see out of my face. And so we hammered in post after post, driving forward a bit, positioning, taking aim, holding the post steady and smashing it in.

It was monotonous work and our progress was slow. I didn't enjoy myself much. Standing barefoot in mud, clinging desperately to fence posts, not even able to swat at the pestering mosquitoes as they tickled and smarted and stung, not even being able to *imagine* anything risky because such a Mennonite Brethren uncle would immediately have seen through me — no, it wasn't my idea of a good time. And all my brother Peter had to do up front was to hold onto the horses, make their eyes reflect his bared teeth and distorted face, talk softly to himself whenever he liked and scratch himself all he wanted. While I stood knee deep in mud, being splattered.

It was fence post Number 23 when it happened. We had just had a little drink of piss-warm water from the syrup pail and I was steadying the post again when I looked over — God only knows why — at Peter, who was gesturing furtively. What he was signalling was that I was supposed to pull the post away at the last moment. Then he disappeared behind the horses. I didn't have much time to think. Uncle Falk had just given the post his initial tap. He was winding up for his haymaker slam; he was already halfway through his swing. His face was a horrible grimace with the effort he was putting into the blow. What could I do? There was really no choice, wouldn't you agree? At the last second I yanked the post away and Uncle Falk came looping from the wagon, following his sledge in a magnificent somersault. His face was twisted with astonishment and fury, and when he landed there was a spectacular explosion of mud, snot, slime and ditch water; everything flew up through the air. The frogs immediately stopped their choir practice, hidden herons burst up from their camouflaged nests, birds scattered through the bushes, and it was all Peter could do to keep the horses from stampeding. And over all this uproar I heard Uncle Falk bellowing at the top of his lungs: "*DEMONS IN SHIT! DEVILS AMONG THE CARROTS!! CHRIST ON A CRUTCH AND THEN SOME!!!*"

Well, when I heard all this I thought I'd better get out of there fast, and I might have gotten away too, except that Uncle Falk had already managed to find his feet and was working hard on a smile and a friendly-look. "Listen, Hansey," he called; "where are you running off to? It was candy I was supposed to bring from Gruenthal, wasn't it? I've got it right here in my pocket." He rummaged around in his overalls and pulled out a handful of something which he stretched out to me, and like a fool I slowly walked up to him and held out my hand.

Well, there's not much more to tell. You can imagine the rest. I, on the other hand, don't have to imagine anything at all, because the memory of the licking he gave me still makes my rear glow like a propane heater whenever I think about it!

("Holy Mister")

All sorts of mischievous things happened in Canada in the Thirties, and not only because people were appallingly poor. Because in those days, people still switched on their imaginative faculties, instead of simply CJOB-FM or CBWT-TV.

So here's the background. As things stood then, there were still more watermelons than churches in southern Manitoba in 1936. That summer Mr. Klassen conducted his own brand of revival meeting in his melon patch behind his house. A year later, Uncle Cornelius Falk applied extravagant heat to my rear for teaching him to fly, and to swear. What followed was Grandfather Krause — Brother Krause, Preacher and Mistah Krause — fastidious and studious in his white shirt and black suit, with a Bible in every pocket.

He had a rosy face and a white goatee, tiny eyes and a thatch of hair that was badly in need of fertilizer. He always had peppermint candies in his vest pockets and a halo on the seat of his pants, and three or four sets of dentures that he carried with him in a little satchel. And he was pious, so pious, but so very, very pious that he even refused to eat the meat of brood sows. That impressed the dickens out of everyone — everyone, that is, but my father, who knew that His Piety had studied in Germany, "and there," my father knew, "people are a little stuck-up and act from the top down." As if to prove father's point, Brother Krause always sat at a separate table from the rest of the family, and received special food. He was "preparing himself for Eternity" he insisted, and so he had to receive a special diet. My father snorted to my mother that he was just trying to fatten himself up.

Have I mentioned that we were so poor during the 1930's that we were still wearing the rags we'd brought along from Russia a dozen years earlier? Well, it's true. We were as poor as Peter Rabbit sitting on a floating stump in the middle of a cold lake with an empty Easter bag on his shivering back.

And so we worked ourselves half to death on that miserable farm, trying to get a few feet ahead. While Preacher Krause sat with his hands clasped prettily over his paunch and twiddled his thumbs. He seemed to have forgotten how to bend down; probably couldn't have if he'd tried. Some people said he'd swallowed a long nail as a child, and that if he bent down he'd do himself inner harm. But when mealtimes were announced, he shot out of his starting gate like a sprinter, making a beeline for the table.

One fine day he called me over and said, "Hans, run fetch two syrup pails. We're going blueberry picking."

"Blueberries?" I puzzled pointedly. "There's no blueberries in the prairies, Grandfather Krause."

"Well, whatever you call them," he grumped, twisting my ear into a painful knot.

So off we went to pick saskatoons for Grandfather Krause's Christmas dinner, a few sealers full he said, and as we walked he told me all about Heaven, and Baptism by immersion, and then he told me an awful lot about Hell, and the second time around he told me only about Hell, until I got the impression that he was probably trying to prepare me for my Eternal Home. And then he told me a little about Germany and then some more about Hell, and then, as we climbed the low hill up to the saskatoon bushes, he told me nothing at all three times in a row, he was breathing so hard, hefting his huge paunch through the Russian thistle.

When we got there we got busy filling our sealers, or I should say *I* got busy filling them, because his berries "always missed the pail" he explained, stuffing great handfuls of them into his mouth. He smacked his lips and slurped up some more, and then he burped and had a look into the syrup pail he'd tied to his huge midriff with a length of binder twine, but there was hardly anything inside. And so I picked into his pail for a while, feeling a bit cheated somehow, until I suddenly spotted a large wasp's nest about five feet above our heads.

Now I'm not going to try to convince you that the idea I got then wasn't Bad and Sinful, but honest, I just wanted to see what would happen. Surely the wasps wouldn't have the nerve to attack as holy a man as Preacher Krause? It was kind of a theological question, the sort of thing one just has to find out. So I picked up a long, dead branch and poked it into the grey nest, and then I told the Preacher I was going to explore a little farther ahead because I thought I remembered some particularly good bushes there.

I didn't have to wait long for my answer. About thirty thousand yellow-jackets felt very strongly about being obliged to settle theological questions on a working day, and they headed straight for Preacher Krause's balding pate. The first thing I heard was a hideous bellow, and then a whirling dervish with dozens of wildly flapping arms appeared out of the saskatoon bushes, the Rogers' syrup pail clanking desperately in hopeless circles. And then my astonished ears heard "Devil!" and then "Son-of-a-bitch!!" and finally "Goddamn in tin cans!!", and then this butterball preacher abruptly developed the speed capability of a supercharged jackrabbit, and he was gone, straight down the hill and across the fields, leaving a smoking trail behind, which I followed much more slowly and contemplatively, marvelling at how interesting Larger Questions could be.

SHOWERS OF BLESSING

(Streume des Sejens)

I was on the verge of closing my car door and taking off when Driediger hollered after me. "Hey, next time you come, how about bringing along a little rain?" He was grinning at me sardonically.

"How much?" I wanted to know.

"Enough for the summerfallow and two laundries. My wife likes to do her washing in rain water."

"Okay," I said. "I'll just see what I can do for all you juiceless Gruenthalers!" And I stepped on the gas.

The next day I searched through an old book from Russia entitled *People, Witches and Their Apprentices* until I found what I was looking for. Under a black-lettered warning NOT FOR AMATEURS OR CHILDREN! was a section on "Rainclouds, Locusts, Cow-Calves and Other Secrets of the Apocalypse." I phoned my old gypsy, the Mazursche, and told her what I had in mind. She cleared her throat and her mind in turn, and then she said thoughtfully: "I think you'd better come around as soon as you can. This calls for a look into my little pot."

And that's what we did. In the meantime it had become so dry that at mealtimes I felt like I was in the Sahara eating grit. Or at Bachelor Aaron Hiebert's eating his pie made with unwashed raisins. Dust ground and puffed and squeaked between my teeth. My stomach gnarled and knotted as if I'd been eating sawdust with bran topped with wood shavings. (The English call that roughage, but where I come from it's known as "roffage", and that's what my neighbour Peters called it as he dragged himself toward the stock trough.)

"Too little water," whispered all my little ducks, hoarse and spent.

But back to the Mazursche. She could see quite clearly now that things were getting serious. She closed her curtains, lit a wreath of candles and opened three books to certain pages. Then she fetched a pile of cards from the corner cupboard. Unfortunately, what she did next is top secret and I'm not allowed to tell you anything about it, but one thing I can tell you is that things in that corner became suddenly very, very hectic. Thunder and lightning erupted from under her blue coverlet — the one with the fringed lace — and then the sparks really started to fly. I shook and trembled and wasn't at all sure I wanted to go on with this, but then I fell flat on my face and she fanned me back to life with her lovely embroidered apron. When that was over, I dragged myself to the corner cupboard, pulled out her bottle of fermented herb juice, and then I let some serious air into that bottle.

I had only just returned home and was getting set to do a little work — when you're the Lord Mayor of Tourond there's always this and that to get done — when the sky began to haze over, and then it darkened, and then it became downright bruised. Inky clouds roiled through the heavens like a gallon of vinegar being poured into a pailful of milk. They spun and swirled, they feinted and panted and groaned, they wrestled and clenched and strained and laboured, working themselves into a celestial sweat. Chickens and cats, dogs and pigs, rabbits and rats, billy-goats and geldings — everything on two or four feet abandoned reality and began scrambling for shelter. Children screamed "Mother!" and dashed inside, hiding under skirts or beds — depending on church affiliation. Old men leafed through the Old Testament and stopped at Daniel, cross-checked various ominous references in Revelations and promised fervently never to misbehave again. The Holdemans, the Church-Of-God-in-Christ Mennonites, even agreed to have nothing more to do with the Yankee-rabblerouser-evangelists from down south. And the Steinbachers promised that if they were spared, they would henceforth vote NDP and speak proper Low German to the end of their days! Yes indeed, that's how authoritative was this Voice from Heaven!

But Driediger? He was still standing out there in Gruenthal, scoffing and scornfully whistling the melody line from "Showers of Blessings". "Big deal," he shrugged.

"Yes yes, that's the way people are," said Mrs. Heinrichs, Harry's mother, who always took her kitchen chair to the beach each summer, and regarded water as nothing special.

Driediger tried to spit in disgust, but only managed a little puff of dust. But a second look at Higher Things slowed him down a little. "Thunderation and gumshoes," he muttered, becoming reflective. Huge clouds were stampeding in from over the cemetery, a pellmell chuckwagon race of wild frothy steeds, green and blue and black and overwhelming.

And then the first waterdrops fell, like air-rifle pellets, like mercury splat. The wind gave everybody a last ten seconds, and then spun around, and the wells of heaven burst open. Driediger was still trying bravely to whistle "Tumbling Tumbleweeds" but it was hopeless. Torrents and cataracts roared from the sky; thunderballs bounded from horizon to horizon; vast sheets of lightning lit the firmament to an intensity that was brighter than day. And the deadly symphony howled its way through all four movements, crescendo and staccato, and mucho-forte everywhere inbetween. . .

And when I tried to phone up Driediger, to ask him his opinion, his wife hemmed and hawed and explained to me that he was fixing the mattress. "He's fixing the mattress," she shouted over the watery din. "He's under there straightening the springcoils; yes, they come loose over the years, you know; it's one of those things that really shows up when the weather starts to turn. . ."

STARS IN THE SKY

(Stearntjes aum Himmel)

"Come a little closer, will you, Hans?" Tina always said when she wanted to hug me. And I always came a little closer and Tina then hugged and kissed me. And strange as it was, whenever anybody else wanted to hug or kiss me, I didn't really want to, but I was always happy when Tina wanted it. Always? Well, to tell the truth it didn't really happen all that often, maybe three or four times a year, at Christmas and on birthdays, and that was about all.

Actually it doesn't really matter how often it did or didn't happen; one's childhood impressions should be allowed to stand. The point is I can still hear her voice saying "Come a little closer, will you, Hans?" as clearly today as if it was fifty years ago. And I hear it often. She always said it so lovingly, with so much heart and soul. And then she laughed, such a beautiful laugh, with little dimples on her cheeks and brow. And Tina laughed often.

Sometimes other people laughed, I mean the adults, when Tina hugged and kissed me. And then I was so embarrassed, I didn't know what to do or how to escape. But my mother told me not to worry about it, that Tina was a good girl, she remembered her well from Russia. . .

Those happy times at Klassens' with Tina and her parents and her brothers and sisters were always as delightful as Christmastime. That was particularly true in winter, when we had to hitch up the horses and drive seven miles and then unhitch them again, and then warm up in the house because we'd all become so fiercely cold during the drive. There was always food and drink, and everybody laughed a lot. And then to come a little closer because Tina wanted to hug and kiss me every now and then. . .

When Tina was as old as I am now, she'd already been dead for fifteen years. And Tina has been gone for a long time, but she still visits me frequently. And then I am always very small and curious and happy and carefree. . . Oh sure, we were all extremely poor during those times, poor devils with old winter coats and worn-out clothes, still wearing leftovers from Russia and lumpy felt boots on our feet. But "we were rich within ourselves" Tina always said, because "when people become outwardly wealthy, they usually wither within."

"How do you know that, Tina?" I asked.

"It's written in all the old stories and books," Tina assured me. "Poor people are rich because they've got lots of time, and rich people are poor because they haven't. It's all in the books and stories."

Time came and time went. And then time started to gallop. But whenever Tina said "Come a little closer, will you, Hans?" time always managed to stand still.

In 1939 I was still a little shaver, it was autumn, I had just returned home from school and was cutting up some pumpkins for cattle feed, when my brother came into the barn and announced that the Second World War had broken out. When I saw Tina not long after she said, "Yes, it's true, now they're fighting in Europe. People can't seem to stop killing each other. They insult each other and they shoot at each other, and the worst of it is, they really seem to *want* to harm each other." I was only eight years old and didn't know what to make of it all. I found it hard to believe because the grown-ups I knew didn't ever behave that way. Though somehow, for some reason, I felt an awful apprehension about it all. But then Tina took me into her arms and kissed me, and all the uneasiness melted away inside. . .

Tina and her sister Lena and her brother Peter and their father began cutting and selling firewood — hundreds of cords of it. Soon everything and anything seemed to be needed and saleable; all of a sudden everybody had money. Tina's father bought a short wave radio, to which he listened all the time, and he always knew everything that Hitler and Churchill had said that day.

Yes, he seemed to know everything. It really was surprising.

A little while later Tina and her sister and her parents went to Winnipeg, to Eaton's, where they had Tina's eyes tested. And then for Christmas, Tina received spectacles. When we met again on Boxing Day, Tina looked so strange, so very strange with those new spectacles. I asked her uneasily whether she really needed to wear those peculiar things, whether she really really had to.

"Come here for a bit, Hans," she said to me, and then she took me outside, onto the front porch.

Out there she showed me all sorts of wonderful things in the sky. The Big Dipper directly overhead, the Little Dipper farther over, and then the North Star by itself.

And then she pointed out how the Dipper always aims at the North Star.

"I knew they all existed," she said softly, "but before I got these spectacles I'd never actually seen them." And she wiped away a tear I hadn't seen before.

But you know, from that evening on, Tina never hugged me again, and I never received another kiss from her. . .

THE COBBLER'S BENCH

(De Reehmabeintj)

In Russia, Peter Neufeld had a large farm and five sons. And he enjoyed the farming well enough, but what he enjoyed even more was making and repairing shoes and harness on his cobbler's bench. "Yes, that's his quirk," said his wife Anna, whom Neufeld always called "Mamme".

On the porch connecting the house and the stable, Neufeld had equipped a tackroom with a sewing machine, a last, a series of hammers and pliers, awls and needles — some crooked, some curved and some straight. He also kept rolls of pitch-yarn there, and his cobbler's apron.

In this room Neufeld worked on harnesses, shoes, house slippers, whatever was made of leather and needed repair. Whenever he wasn't in the fields or couldn't be found anywhere else, that's where he was bound to be. During the winter or after the day's work was done, he cobbled and sewed "until his snot caught fire" in the irreverent words of a fellow Mennonite Brethren member, who took care to remain anonymous because one's repairs tended to take a little longer if such remarks came full circle.

Yes, this was where Neufeld was truly at home. No matter what anxieties might be bothering him or what troubles loomed, when he sat down at his cobbler's bench he became a new man, a relaxed, cheerful free spirit. In no time at all he would begin to sing, Russian songs and German songs: "I Pray To The Power of Love", "Die Lorelei", "Youth, Beautiful Youth", but best of all he liked to sing "Often In The Circle of My Beloved". He often assembled all five sons in the cobblery, and then they sang fit to raise the roof. And Neufeld smiled. He sang and smiled. Other people usually just sang while working in the fields, when day's end was approaching and the insects were diminishing, and the horses had caught their second wind and were more willing again. And Neufeld sang then too, sang enthusiastically and melodiously to his two horses, Orlik and Mashka, who pricked their ears and kept better time as they did. But most of all, Neufeld liked to sing in his cobblery.

Well, times came and times went, and then time started to gallop. Suddenly there were dark clouds on the horizon, and they wouldn't go away. Then there was thunder and lightning, of an evil kind that no wind seemed able to move and no prayer alter. A malignant darkness set in over the Mennonite villages of the Ukraine. . .

For the next half-dozen years Neufeld consoled himself constantly with this thought: "Things will be alright, eventually. Just have patience. Patience." And he kept on farming and cobbling and singing as best as circumstances would permit. Often, circumstances didn't. And as one son after another fled to Canada, his singing became sadder and quieter and less frequent. The sons wrote back often at first, long accounts of the freedoms and riches in this new land, but then they seemed to have become rich themselves, too rich and too busy, yes, far too busy and their letters arrived less and less often. And then they stopped arriving at all.

Neufeld kept farming, but his farming now proceeded as unenthusiastically as his sewing machine. His cobbler's hammer remained untouched on his leather apron for days and weeks, and his spectacles remained in his vest pocket. And the singing? Well, only on Sundays in church. And finally he took to idling away long hours in the cobblery, doing nothing at all. He seemed a little lost. His wife, now called Anna since the children had left, tried now and then to lift his spirits by singing "Often in the Circle of My Beloved" and Neufeld did try to join in, but his heart wasn't in it and he usually faded away. Sometimes Anna showed him snapshots of their grandchildren in Canada: "See? That's Kennett, that's Heater, and there at the back is Cattrien, all Peter's children." But Neufeld didn't even bother to put on his spectacles. "They don't even know German," he shrugged. . . and went to bed.

Hunger and sorrow now knocked regularly on Neufeld's door. Neufeld spent much time brooding, questioning his fate. How was this all possible? How could God forget his own children so callously? Eventually patience could no longer sustain even the patient Neufeld. He and Anna packed a few small possessions and joined the throngs of the fleeing. And arrived in Canada, eventually, to join their children, their grandchildren and who knew what else. . .

For a short time after their arrival, Neufeld's sails seemed to catch a breeze. But his new fate was overwhelming. What direction should he take now? Where was he to find a new home in this huge country? His own children had become strangers to him. Oh certainly, they offered room and board, but somehow it was not enough. Anna said very little, but you could see she was having the same problem. "I think I'm too old for this country," she said finally, her chin trembling. "I'm homesick." And then she lay down and folded her hands and wept. She looked for her apron, but she couldn't find it. Worse than that, she didn't really need it anymore. "Anna is gone," was all that Neufeld said. And whether people here or there or anywhere else had any more luck in squaring themselves away he didn't know, but somehow this country wasn't an easy fit. But then again, what was the point of such thoughts, Neufeld thought to himself. What was the point of thinking?

After the funeral, Abraham and John and Peter and Isaac got together. For the first time since they'd come to Canada, it seemed, they found the time, they made time to reflect on the image of their father, standing alone at the grave turning the brim of his black hat over and over in his hands. He was as much a stranger to them now as they to him; how had this all managed to happen? Who would have thought that it would all come to this? Yes it was true, they had all been too busy, far too busy. . .

So it was decided to move him to Peter's place in Gnadenfeld. To move in there with Peter and Agatha. Anna's effects remained to be dealt with, of course, and his few possessions too; but in two weeks they would return and accomplish this. They all agreed on it.

Two weeks later they all showed up at the appointed time. And when they arrived at Peter's farm in Gnadenfeld, take a guess at what had been set up between the house and the barn, in a little room on the porch. Yes, a fully equipped cobblery, with a new cobbler's bench and every cobbling tool imaginable.

Old Peter Neufeld sat himself down on that cobbler's bench and made himself good and comfortable. Then he picked up the hammer, filled his mouth with nails and began to drive them experimentally into the heel of an old boot. And then he set the sewing machine into motion and then he pounded some more nails, and soon he was cobbling and sewing as if his snot had caught fire. And suddenly all six Neufeld sons and half a dozen wee Neufelds and also Agatha and two other daughters-in-law burst into "Often in the Circle of My Beloved".

Well, you might say time stopped, and then time reversed, and then it started galloping backwards. Old Neufeld looked over his glasses and then he looked through them, and then he had just a thing or two to say. About how he felt pretty comfortable, about how it felt all right in this new home he was in, not too bad, really, not too bad at all. And Neufeld sewed and he sang a little more, and then he sang and he sewed. And now and then he hammered in a few more little nails and smiled. . .

IN COURT

(Verem Jerecht)

Wellem Pankratz came to Canada in 1926 and do you know where he settled? He settled where he shouldn't have, in Gopherville, sixty miles west of Mousetown — which is to say, on the Other Side. Pankratz's neighbours were Mennonites too, "but only *Kanadiers*" according to Pankratz, "and they're either hypocrites or they're boors." As for their education, they had "damn little" by Pankratz's standards. I told Pankratz he shouldn't be saying such things, and he agreed, but he said he'd say them anyway. Well, nobody likes to be called a fool, not even the *Kanadiers,* and so they squared with Pankratz in their own way.

When Pankratz built himself a garage, the neighbours' boys left their footprints in the wet concrete during the night. When Pankratz set up his brood hens, the boys put stones among the eggs. One morning Neighbour Pankratz woke up to find all his horses without their tail hair, which the boys had sold to a sofa-maker in town. All this, as you might imagine, got Pankratz mighty incensed. "Those horses look like old fat women in short skirts," he fumed. "Especially my old gelding, Orlik. Just look at him! He's downright ashamed of that crooked whisk on his muffler!"

You might ask how Pankratz made out on Hallowe'en night — and that's the right question. Because the boys pushed over Pankratz's biffy with Pankratz in it, which really got him sore. "I can't understand it," he groused. "I a man who even managed to teach the Communists some manners, and now I can't even seem to touch this rabble. Well, we'll just see about that!"

Pankratz proceeded to resurrect himself and his biffy, found his overalls needed changing, and then hid in his barn until dark. The neighbourhood boys showed up right on schedule. As they snuck past the barn, Pankratz swooped out like an avenging angel hollering, "Hah! There you are, you miserable dung beetles! Now I've got you!" The boys ran for their lives and they all managed to get away, all except Old Giesbrecht's Willie, who stumbled and fell and then became the recipient of the sound thrashing Pankratz had been supremely anxious to give away that night. You might assume that Pankratz conducted that thrashing with the flat of his hand, and maybe he did and maybe he didn't — we'll clarify that point a little later on in the story.

So Old Giesbrecht naturally phoned the police. He swore up and down he was going to "settle up", and when the police arrived they duly noted young Willie's black and blue spots, served Pankratz with a warrant, and so four weeks later this whole passel of pacifists and conscientious objectors found themselves gathered in court to have it out.

Now this sort of excitement wasn't available every day, so as you might imagine, the court room was filled to the rafters. There was Squint-eyed Buhler, Whisky-Sawatsky and all his gang; there was Peter Wieler with his rascal offspring, Peter Penner from Plum Coulee, and in the second row Storyteller John Janzen and Roughy-

Thiessen. Cucumber-Wiebe and Turkey Wiens were there, predictably; they wouldn't have missed this for anything. And at the back sat Paul Peter's Anna and Stubborn Nickel's Franz, while Solomon Schroeder, the songster, as usual had to park himself in the very first row.

And then it began. The non-Mennonite judge came in, "black as a Hutterite", and everybody stood up and then sat down. Left of the judge sat Willem Pankratz, and to his right Old Giesbrecht's Willie, his ball cap in his hand. And a whole courtroom full of *Kanadiers* and scoffers.

"So that's how it goes with you peace-loving church-goers, eh?" said the judge. "You left Russia because you didn't want to fight, and here you're right away into each other's business like a bunch of dirty shirts. Seems to me there's a little straightening out needed around here." And he turned to the accused on his left and cleared his throat. "Well, Mister Pankratz, these kids have been bothering you a little, have they? A little teasing, a little razzing, shall we call it?"

"Yessir!" Pankratz agreed.

"And you, young Giesbrecht, you claim Mr. Pankratz gave you a whack with his fist or a club?"

"That's right," Willie bleated. "Not once, but a bunch of times, and then he said he'd give my dad a poke in the nose while he was at it, and if he ever catched me again he'd make sure I didn't walk for at least three weeks!"

That didn't sound too good for Pankratz, and Pankratz began to rock back and forth in his seat, with his head shaking a bit like a loose trailer-hitch, winking and blinking in an odd sort of way.

"I'm afraid, Mr. Pankratz," said the judge, "that you don't seem to have fully realized you're no longer among the socialist lawbreakers of Russia. We run a civilized society here in this country. In Canada you don't just hit first and sort things out later. I believe this court will have to teach you more democratic manners." Old Giesbrecht and Willie started to grin, enjoying their upcoming victory. "Am I making you nervous, Mr. Pankratz? Is there any particular reason why you're shaking the way you are?"

"That comes from the war," Pankratz quavered apologetically. "I fought for the Whites against the Communists, and they threw me in a P.O.W. camp and they starved and tortured us. I've just never gotten over it, I mean my nervous system."

The judge's eyebrows rose sharply. "You fought the Communists in the last war? The Reds? And served a term in a P.O.W. camp?"

Pankratz could only nod helplessly, obviously trying to suppress the spasmodic shaking of his jowls. His hands twitched, and his eyes rolled like a molasses barrel down a milk-can ramp.

"This may require a fuller examination," the judge decided, banging his gavel on a wooden block. "Court adjourned for a recess. And you, Mr. Pankratz, I'll see you immediately in my chambers."

So the bailiff helped Pankratz into the judge's private back room and Pankratz had to tell his story to the judge, not once but twice, and then they had a companionable smoke. And when they re-entered the courtoom, the judge had a much clearer grasp of the situation.

"Were there any witnesses to this alleged remonstration with this ill-behaved Giesbrecht lad? Anyone who actually saw it happen? Nobody? I thought not. The point is, Willie Junior, that such leftist behaviour should and needs to be corrected, and if you received such correction from Mr. Pankratz's hands, you should be thanking him rather than trying to vilify him in court. I will not castigate a man for taking upon himself what another's parents or teachers have lamentably neglected to provide. And if a hammer handle was the only rod available at that moment, so be it; we cannot always expect of life that it provide us with perfect solutions for unexpected problems.

"And so the court demands an apology from Willie Giesbrecht and applauds Wellem Pankratz's sense of social responsibility. His actions constitute the essence of a working democracy. As for you parents in the audience, if you find any of your own children demonstrating this kind of leftist behaviour, I can only hope and suggest that you not spare the rod and make it necessary for Wellem Pankratz to defend democracy again. This court is dismissed."

ANNIE, LIE STILL!

(Auna, Lidj Stell)

Now, if you ladies will all sit down, and you, Esther, hurry up and fetch us some sunflower seeds, I'll tell you all about Old Peter Hiebert, whom we used to call Bachelor-Hiebert or Pipe-Hiebert — you know, the one who was kicked out of the Eden Mennonite Church.

Now Hiebert was still one of the *Russlaender*, born over there but brought to Canada as an eight-year-old little shaver, and my Lord was he an imp! For example, on their way by ship from Moorhead, North Dakota to Winnipeg on the Red River, little Peterkin went missing, there was a huge uproar, and everybody started searching for the child. The ship was halted, the side-wheels creaked and then stood still, Mrs. Hiebert was already crying bitterly into her handkerchief and Old Man Hiebert spat angrily overboard, saying, "Son-of-a-bitch!" Mrs. Prune Sawatsky, as you can imagine, lost no time in telling her story about a similar little boy who'd drowned in the Dnieper river, and then she pointed out that that's what happens when you don't tan young boys' hides more regularly. That was Mrs. Sawatsky's resolute opinion. Meanwhile nobody was managing to come up with Peterkin, which convinced Old Man Hiebert he might have to take a good look around himself.

It wasn't long before Old Hiebert bellowed out so loud, you could hear him all over the ship.

"Thunderation and petticoats! Cuckoos in the clocks and herons in the sorrel! There he is, the little water rat!!" And sure enough: there was Peter, swimming cheekily in the Red River! "By God and by golly!" the old man hollered, bright red in the face, "you get out of there this instant, immediately and on the spot!! What the hell do you think you're doing? We're on our way to Canada for God's sake; there may be Indians up there waiting to be skinned, and you're wasting everybody's time with a Saturday bath in this mudpuddle of a buffalo trough!! Now get out of there and back into your pants, or I'll brand your buns with the Stars and Stripes on each side! And you, Penner, you tell the Captain to fire up the steam; we haven't got all day!"

Yes, that was Hiebert's Peterkin, and when he got to Canada the pranks did not diminish. They say he was naughtier than the Old Original Adam himself, who was also up to no good in the apple patch, as Old Man Hiebert used to put it. But Peterkin said he had only been playing Indian because he'd been told they were even wilder than Wild Wiens from some village or other in Russia; that's what people had told him.

Well, anyway, Hiebert's Peterkin was and remained a prankster. And that brings me to what I really wanted to tell you about him, but I'm not even sure I should — well, okay, I will, but you've all got to promise that this story will never go beyond this room! Do you all promise? Especially you, Mrs. Panner; those stories you tell about the Peter Thiessens in Gnadenfeld are always terribly exaggerated. Oh no, I don't just think that, I know what I know. Besides, if this story's ever to be told again, I'll do the telling myself, is that understood? You promise? All right then, I'll go on.

So have you ever wondered about the *real* reason that Bachelor Hiebert was kicked out of the Eden Mennonite Church? Well, I just happen to know the reason. Because I always wondered why Hiebert was always so secretive when it came to women. People tried for months to find out what he was up to after hours, and he was up to something, that much was for sure. Old Mrs. Barthel told me so, and she's rarely wrong in matters of that kind.

So one fine Sunday he was sitting in church and it was the Reverend Jantzen preaching, you know, the long-winded one who always repeats himself. And after a while, at first you could only hear it very quietly, and then louder and louder, it was Bachelor Hiebert snoring like a buzz-saw. So the Reverend Jantzen started talking louder too, about how Cain smote Abel with a crowbar across his back, and then across his head too, I suppose, because you can't really kill someone by just hitting them across the back, can you? And all the while Bachelor Hiebert was still sitting there between Peter Loewen and Tobias Janz, just smiling dreamily and snoring like a double bass in action: *Ppiirrrrhhh! Ppiirrrhhh!!* And finally it was all too much for Janz. After all, they *were* in church. So he let Bachelor Hiebert have it with a hefty nudge in the ribs. Bip! just like that, and Hiebert gave a sort of sigh and then he said really loudly, so you could hear it five rows back, he said: "Annie, lie still!"

THE BRIDAL GOWN

(Daut Bruttjleed)

Uncle Cornelius hailed from Einlage, in Russia. Like most Einlagers, he was a lively fellow, snappy and not exactly shy. When he walked up or down the village street, his coat-tails always seemed to swing with a little extra flair. Oh yes, he cut a fine figure with the ladies, this young dentist. "A devastating suitor," said the women. "A dreamy guy," observed the girls, and "A haughty cock," was the boys' assessment.

Then one fine day the swaggering and strutting stopped. Uncle Cornelius had fallen in love. Oh yes, very much in love, and it clipped his wings a little. But not long afterwards he had himself a bride. And what a bride! Greta was a beautiful and happy girl, bright and intelligent, with a good heart. And soul? By the binful. Eyes? All of Russia was reflected in them.

Their happiness, however, was soon beset by clouds. Revolution overwhelmed Russia, and the dogs of war tore and mauled the country like a soupbone. Greta Redekopp's father scanned the horizon, didn't like what he saw coming, and decided it was time to pull up stakes. He decided to head for Canada.

Uncle Cornelius wasn't entirely convinced. He decided to stay in Russia for another six months, in case things got better. If they did, his bride Greta would return; if not, he would follow her to Canada. In either case, they would be married within the half-year, whether in Russia or in Canada. . .

I won't even try to describe their farewell on August 23, 1928. Anyone who's experienced such agony will know what I'm talking about. For those who haven't, words would be hopelessly inadequate. Greta and Cornelius were dumb and almost paralyzed with grief. "Adieu, my sweet Cornelius; don't forget my eyes. I love you."

"Goodbye Greta, take my heart and this parcel with you to Canada."

It wasn't long before the lights went out in Russia, and they didn't come back on again for 17 years. Everywhere there was more fear than love, and more suspicion than trust.

And Cornelius and Greta?

Cornelius had a nephew in Canada, whom I met in Germany many years later. I asked him about his uncle back in Einlage. He was quiet for a long time and then he said: "Strange, you know, even puzzling, that I've never been able to talk about this in Canada, while in Germany I'm almost anxious to spill it out." He pursed his lips thoughtfully, and then he shrugged and told this tale:

You see, Uncle Cornelius had studied dentistry here; he'd almost decided to stay here actually, but then he found himself missing the steppes, the Dnieper, the sun and his people. So he went back, and he found himself a gorgeous girl named Greta.

Now Uncle Cornelius thought like most Mennonites did: that Communism was just a temporary cloud on the horizon. But of course it turned out to be more, much more. And Greta's father didn't trust the look of things at all, right from the beginning, and he was one of the first to pack up and leave. "They're going to clean our clocks in Russia, you bet your life! And it won't just be because of our religion," he warned. "We've been treating the peasants around here like toilet paper."

That statement proved a heavy mortgage for Redekopp in Manitoba, Canada. The Mennonites there decided that was Communist talk, or at least the closest thing to it. But of course they didn't have the nerve to say anything to him directly; they just accused him of it behind his back. He didn't discover the true shape of things until he applied for membership in his local church and was told by the church elders to "first confess everything".

"I never stooped while I was in Russia, and I'm not going to start now," Redekopp informed them, and he packed up again and moved to a German settlement in southwestern Saskatchewan. "And if anyone wants my address, they can enquire of God. Goodbye." Meanwhile, back in Russia, the gates and doors of the nation clanged shut both inside and out. Shut, closed and sealed. "And that's it for you," the Russians told Cornelius.

So Cornelius sat there in Einlage, waiting and yearning and worrying himself sick. All he wanted to do was go to Canada to join Greta. And his life swung perpetually between two polarities: hope and despair. Now the former had the upper hand, now the latter. Sometimes he was sure it would all work out; other times he was bleak with despondency. And so it went on and on. He knew that Greta would be faithful to him, his heart told him that. But by now, no one could tell him where she'd gone. Occasionally some small snippet of news or purported news drifted over, but that was all. No mail was getting through in either direction.

And Greta? Well, she was waiting on a farm halfway between Liebenthal and Rastatt in southwestern Saskatchewan. Waiting and waiting. Eventually Old Redekopp got a job managing a small grain elevator and they managed to survive, after a fashion. Greta wrote every week and planted flowers for her wedding and a myrtle plant for her wedding wreath. The following year she did it all again, and the next year, and the next. . . And it's anybody's guess how often she tried on that wedding dress Cornelius had given her — because that's what had been in that parcel, you know.

Uncle Cornelius's nephew stopped talking for a while. We were sitting at a window in an old pub, the Niedlingsmuehle, and the evening lights were glinting luxuriously off the wineglasses and the wine bottle on the table. There was a basket of fresh bread and a tiny butter-crock beside the salt-grinder.

Well, of course you know what happened next — the terrible famine throughout Russia, and all the Mennonite families in the Ukraine torn apart, and then war broke out. It wasn't long before the Germans arrived in Einlage. The German army set up its headquarters in Uncle Cornelius's house because it was big and Uncle Cornelius had some medical knowledge, and he spoke good German. Plus he was known to be a reasonable enough fellow.

But the war turned around in 1943 and one evening the German major confided to Uncle Cornelius that they'd be retreating over the Dnieper the next day. "Tell only your best friends. They can come along too. Tomorrow at ten, and you'd better be ready. Anybody who doesn't cross the river with us will be stuck here for good, because we're dynamiting the bridge. The Russians are very close."

There was no decision to be made at the news — Uncle Cornelius was more desperate to get out of Einlage than anyone else. But before leaving he had an urgent matter to attend to, and he was having difficulty getting clear of the German officer, who had a thousand things to prepare and needed Uncle Cornelius's help to accomplish them. The evening evaporated, then the night. At eight-thirty the next morning the Germans began to retreat over the bridge and at nine-fifteen the last transports were rolling across, and still Uncle Cornelius hadn't found the opportunity to settle his own affairs.

The last German officers urged him to hurry. When they had gone, Uncle Cornelius ran to his orchard, spade in hand, paused briefly to get his bearings, then made straight for a particular apple tree and began frantically to dig. Sod flew, then earth, and then gravel — uncooperative, hard-frozen gravel. Uncle Cornelius attacked the ground like a man possessed. And the harder he dug, the faster the time seemed to fly. Ten o'clock was the deadline, the officer had told him. At ten o'clock they'd be blowing up the bridge. At ten to ten Uncle Cornelius finally found what he was looking for: ten pounds of gold, his gold reserves for filling teeth, buried in a canvas bag under this apple tree. He flung the gold into a travelling bag, hurled in some buns and whatever other food came quickly to hand, threw the bag over his shoulder and sprinted for the bridge. Those who saw him said they'd never seen a man run so fast. The Germans on the other side saw him too and some shouted, "Hurry up man, faster, faster!" while others yelled, "Back man, back!!"

Then the bridge blew up — just as Uncle Cornelius got to it. They tell me he slammed to a stop and threw himself backwards, but whether that's true, or whether he was wounded by the blast, or whether the Reds got him, gold and all, nobody knows. All I know is that Uncle Cornelius was never seen or heard from again.

And Greta?

That autumn, when we got back from Germany, Uncle Cornelius's nephew and I drove out past Liebenthal. We asked around, searched in a grid pattern, asked again. "Maybe one of those deserted houses near the old grain elevator, down there on the spur line," an old-timer suggested. All the names had been changed to English, but the elevator was still there. Its windows were all broken and the roof let in the sky. Its grain spout creaked eerily back and forth in the wind, moaning with each gust. It was enough to make you shudder, but we wanted to find out what had happened. "Tell us what you know," I wanted to say to these sad, abandoned buildings. "Tell us about all those who worked here and laughed here and cried here. Show us where they hoped, and where they doubted." But there was no answer. We went on to search three adjacent, empty houses and found nothing. There was a fourth, a two-storeyed one at the back, with a few wild flowers and some dill still blooming bravely in the garden — its roof caved in but its chimney still standing.

We pushed our way inside; the door was unlocked. There seemed little of any interest. An old stove with crooked little legs in the kitchen; a faded calendar on the wall, and an old edition of the Eaton's catalogue in a corner cupboard. That was all.

"Might try the upstairs," I suggested, and Uncle Cornelius' nephew gave a tug at the stairway door.

At first it wouldn't give. And then it did. And that's where we found it, right behind that door, on a wooden hanger grey with age. A long, white wedding dress, with lace and frills and beautiful puffed sleeves — old but not worn out. On the collar below the lace were some letters embroidered in blue silk thread. They read: "G.R. from C.T."

And that was all.

(Trajchtmoakasch)

What is a Mennonite, you ask? I mean a *real* Mennonite, an unmistakable Mennonite? Well, that's a tough question, a very tough question. Mennonites who haven't been able to answer it to other Mennonites' satisfaction over the centuries have often been catapulted unceremoniously out of the Mennonite orbit. Yes, even booted out, like a football, and the place-kickers were generally inflated Ministers of the Word, or mobs of angry church-gangsters. Yes yes, and the boots weren't Adidas either, but General Conference Specials or Mennonite Brethren Hardliners.

But that isn't answering the question, which I'll do forthwith, if you'll just turn off the TV and give me a moment of your time. A Mennonite is this: a person of the human persuasion who speaks Low German and who patronizes a bonesetter. Yes, that's right; a bonesetter.

What bonesetters, you may ask; who are these people and where do they hide out? Well, usually at the end of the village or a short distance into the bush, more or less out of sight. And they are almost always the objects of a certain fashionable scorn. Nobody takes them seriously until they're needed, and then, of course, they're everyone's best friend, buddy, relative and bosom pal. (This was particularly true before Medicare!) "Oh sure, I know him well, even from Russia yet, or from Altona."

And then off he goes, our unmistakable Mennonite, to have his bones shaken back into place, and if the sprain is particularly bad, he'll swear never again to malign the profession. Yes, he'll even promise to leave behind three or five dollars in payment, if only his limbs are restored once more. But the bonesetter has never made more than a very modest living out there in the bush, because the 1936 version of our unmistakable Mennonite promised inwardly to leave a quarter but always, once he could walk again, left only a dime, and the 1990's version promises fervently to leave a five-spot but rarely leaves more than a few coins or a few singles. "Well, it's not real work anyways," he says to himself; "and one shouldn't spoil these lazy rascals by being too generous — it'll just fill their heads with silly notions."

A bonesetter is usually of the male persuasion. If female, she must be comparatively old and of husky build. No true Mennonite would visit a skinny, bony, female bonesetter. And they're called Trutje, Doctah Abram Peters, Doctah Wire-Burner Friesen, Fat-Belly Hildebrandt, Willems Jake, Lady Ginter, Plum Panner or Dove-Dyck.

A bonesetter shouldn't take anything under advisement, consult with colleagues, be unsure of the diagnosis or any of those other modern forms of medical foolishness. If he doesn't know or can't form an opinion instantly, he has no business being in the business. He should always begin by viciously attacking the backbone and unravelling its knots, because everybody knows that without healthy vertebrae, a man is merely a snake with legs. The neck should always be massaged until a clearly audible *gnups* is heard. Arms, fingers, chest, neck;

everything accessible should be rubbed with liniment or spirits or carbolic salve, while the bonesetter keeps a constant accompaniment of: "See? It stinks and stings, but that's how you tell it's working," followed by questions about whether your father still barters chickens and old hens, and whether Giesbrecht's Willie is still the mischievous scoundrel he was last year, and whether the Holdemann Mennonites will also go to heaven. He may inform you that Mrs. Peter Schellenberg has cancer because she's been drinking her coffee too hot, yes, much too hot for years now, and incidentally, where did you get that lump on your shoulder, the left one, here, right here. "You took a terrible fall when you were a child, have I got it right?"

"That's right."

"Well, see, I knew that all along because I felt it as soon as I laid hands on you. So from now on you'll have to take it nice and easy, especially when bending down to thump watermelons. And no more wrestling with that billy-goat of yours you call Oskar Ayatollah. Okay then, enough for today. Come back if you hear any unusual noises in your bones, and remember, you're not the youngest anymore, okay? And you can pay me whatever you want to."

Which is exactly what the unmistakable Mennonite does, and that brings me to my second and closing definition: At pay-up time, a Mennonite is a person of the human persuasion whose billfold usually contracts a bad case of constipation.

MERRY CHRISTMAS

(Froobe Wiebnacht)

I had to promise old Johann Rempel that I wouldn't tell this story to anyone until he'd gone "upstairs". Now he's up there, and I may — indeed I must — tell you Johann Rempel's Christmas story.

"Exactly why," Rempel had been asking for years, "exactly why do I have so much trouble getting into the spirit of Christmas these days? What's wrong with me, or with the world?"

And then old Uncle Rempel began to tell us how beautiful Christmas had always been at home on the Dnieper River, how happy everyone was then, and how all of Nature managed to come to rest on Christmas Eve and during the Christmas holidays, to express its gratitude and to shout "Merry Christmas!" in all directions. Yes, everyone did that; everyone shouted "Merry Christmas!" and the word spread like a warm chinook for thousands of miles through the night. And people took to liking each other again, started talking to each other once more. "In Low German, of course," Uncle Rempel pointed out. "And if they really straightened things out between them, then the wind had no trouble at all carrying the message of Merry Christmas in all directions.

"But today? Just look at all this fearful haste and panic. People drive themselves crazy, they harass themselves to the point of nervous breakdowns, and never even get close to achieving the happiness they're chasing after. And that, of course, is why you never see any angels anymore." Old Uncle Rempel was so moved by all this tragedy that he had to pull out his handkerchief and dab at his eyes a little.

Then he got up to leave. But at the door he turned around once more and suggested: "You know, I think we've become too addicted to progress. We're afraid of missing out on the smallest thing. We feel we have to take part in everything. I think we've simply put far too much on our plates." And then he walked off in that thoughtful way of his. Somehow very slow, very alone, very lonely. He couldn't seem to feel at home in his own house anymore, and that made me very sad, because Uncle Rempel had always been a man who'd had a pretty good idea how things fitted together.

Last Christmas, on December 23, old Johann Rempel suddenly appeared on my doorstep, but this time he was astonishingly full of excitement, joy and energy. "Listen to this," he said to me. "I had a dream the other night that I really have to tell you. I dreamed," he went on without pausing, undoing his coat buttons and pulling off his hat, "I dreamed that I was in a large room, a very large room and everything was very bright and trimmed in blue. Somebody was playing Mozart, with one harp following another, and it was wonderfully pleasant, really lovely. It felt just like home. And Greta was there and immediately came over, told me about the marvelous rusks they baked there, and how Jacob Thiessen's Missus from Einlage was making her scrumptuous whiteloaf again. Yes, and I met Uncle Tobias Janz and Franz

Guenther too, and Janz wanted to play a game of chess with me right on the spot, and Guenther showed me the beautiful pictures he'd painted. Yes sir, I visited them all and we talked a blue streak; it was as good as way back then, on the Dnieper, when I was just a little shaver. And then, after I'd finished a game of chess and had my fill of those delicious rusks baked in the old-colony way, the Chief of the Angels came over to me, patted me on the back and asked: 'Could you spare me a moment of your time, Uncle Rempel?'

"Well, that gave me a bit of a start, of course; first, because I could now see that angels really did exist; and second, because this Head Angel spoke such perfect Low German; and third, because this magnificent specimen of Angel had actually addressed me by name. Who would have imagined such a thing?

"So there I was at the Chief Angel's side, with everybody waving and greeting us on all sides. We headed off to the big parlour, where they made me comfortable and brought in all sorts of delicacies, anything my heart desired. The servants were apprentice angels with very small wings and beautiful eyes; most of them had blonde braids and teeth as white and regular as rice. And their clothes? Well, their clothes were mostly sky-blue, with pompoms. And they all ran around barefoot. And polite! — it was like in Sunday school. And did I mention their Low German? As perfect as only someone from the *Molotschna* could speak it. And then all those little ones curtsied and skipped away.

"Well and then the Head Angel said to me: 'My dear Rempel, this is really a pleasure. I've been wanting to speak to you for some time. Because I've been hearing about your concerns for the people of the Earth at Christmastime, and I want you to know that you're absolutely right. The people down there have lost their individualism, we can see that very clearly from up here, and we can deal with that to some extent, but there is one thing even we have found ourselves powerless to counteract: Mennonite industriousness. This industriousness tends to display two particularly worrisome characteristics: first, because the industrious Mennonite is usually chasing after real estate and ever more real estate, his gaze is almost permanently directed toward the ground. And second, all this gazing at the ground depresses his vocal cords, and after a while he can't speak Low German anymore. And once he stops speaking Low German, of course, he's completely lost his unique identity. And all this because of his ridiculous Mennonite industriousness. So I'm afraid we've had to decide to break off relations with those sorts of Mennonites; we're not sending them any angels any more. Now I'm not saying this means they can't get to heaven — a few of them do seem to manage it — but those who do usually have to take a couple of months of refresher courses out in the anteroom, before their lovely colourful Low-German feathers begin to grow back. Because you can always recognize the unilingual Mennonite, you know: with those drab dirty-grey feathers, he always looks like a plain ordinary sparrow.

'So that's how it is, Johann. And now, do you have any questions for us?'

'Just one,' I answered. 'What job do you do up here?'

'I'm responsible for Time,' the Head Angel told me. 'I *am* Time. I'm the Judge of Time.'

'And so, Johann,' the Head Angel continued, 'I'd like you to go back to Manitoba and everywhere else where there are Mennonites, and I'd like you to tell them what it's like up here, and how things stand. And you tell them that they're only going to gain back the Christmas spirit through the Low German language. If they get back to that, we'll do our part and send them our messenger, the Christmas Angel, once again. Feel free to pass on to everyone you meet — in Low German, of course — our message of Good Cheer and a Merry Christmas — we appreciate that sort of thing up here. And when you've accomplished all that, you may return to us; we're keeping your place for you.'

"So Merry Christmas!" Uncle Rempel grinned, and he was gone.

ADAM, WHERE ARE YOU?

("Adam, wo best Du?")

With grateful thanks and a hat tip to
Nicholas Neufeld, whose early version of a similar
idea constitutes the genesis of this story.

It was a beautiful Sunday afternoon in May, the sweet smell of Spring was in the air, the sun dripped its golden taffy on the little town of Einlage on the Dnieper River, and everywhere life was stirring anew. Even old Horse-Hiebert was on the move; he had been gone for three days already, visiting the village of Arkadak; the towns-people gossipped that he was courting once more.

Well, and why not? His wife had died almost two years previously, and there had been meagre pickings from the kitchen since then, and a bit "lonely in the bedroom too", to hear him tell it.

So: Hiebert was in Arkadak, his daughters and the hired help at home, and little Peter, Peterkin, the twelve-year-old ne'er-do-well too clever for his own good — that little Peter was hanging around the village down by the river, wondering what to do with himself, prepared for anything — even, if need be, a little mischief. He wasn't interested in playing with girls, heck no, better to just harass some chickens if it came to that, maybe sneak some eggs out of some crows' nests, that kind of thing. Yes, today he felt ready for all kinds of heroics, but what should they be, exactly? A tough question, no doubt about it, but if you'll make yourself comfortable and lend an ear, I'll tell you in detail what this little rascal managed to cook up.

First he headed over to the Peters', but Victor, little Vicky, was more interested in reading books than in brewing up trouble with Peterkin. So Peter angled back across the street to the Derksens', the Sunflower-Cracker Derksens. True, his father had forbidden him to go there, but he was itching for a little action, he needed some excitement, and there was Derksen's Willi conveniently coming out of the house.

Willi was already fifteen, "crude as Rasputin" in Peter's father's estimation. "You just watch yourself around that scalawag, my boy!" But today Peter approached him brashly, shouting: "Hey Willi! So what are you up to over there today? Cracking sunflower seeds, or still sleeping?"

Willi instantly bent down to look for a stone. But Peter was ready for him. He scooped up a big one, wound up and fired it, bullseye, through the fence pickets, catching Willi square in the solar plexus. There was a muffled thud, a little puff of dust from Willi's shirt, and then the older boy groaned and sagged to the ground. "Oh boy oh boy oh man," Peter thought to himself. "I'm not even thirteen yet, and you could already call me Cain." No sir, there's no place in heaven for boys like that, Preacher Epp had told them last week in Sunday school.

Peter peered thoughtfully through the fence at the motionless Willi. The world was suddenly looking rather grim. And then this grim world became even gloomier when the door opened again and old Sunflower-Cracker Derksen Senior stepped out. There he stood in his enormous entirety: big, fat, glowering, ill-humoured and still in his slippers. He scratched his chest, cleared his throat with a peremptory "ahem!" and then shoved off to inspect the prone Willi. "What's going on here then — epileptic fits or bullshit?" He lifted the boy like a sack and dragged him into the porch. At this Willi regained consciousness and began to wail: "No no, no epileptic, no epileptic, it was Horse-Hiebert's Petey, he wapped me in the gut with a rock, he's still standing outside there!"

"Aha! Ahem. Well, we'll just see about that, won't we?" the old seed-gnasher groused. He immediately pulled out his pocket-knife, stepped down the stairs and relieved an adjacent acacia bush of a long, supple switch. It only took about a minute. Meanwhile young Peter was still standing there, still entranced by his Sunday school dilemma, still rooted to the spot. His eyes darted in all directions, his tongue moistened his lips anxiously, and his heart bonged like an empty barrel in a delivery cart.

Uncle Derksen advanced on him slowly, step by step, as if intuiting the boy's confusion. He shook his switch gently, whistled soothingly as if calming a cornered animal, his glittering eyes sure of victory, muttering: "If old Horse-Hiebert can't keep a bridle on his son, I suppose I'll just have to throw a rope on him myself!" Only four more steps. . . three. . . he reached with his left hand, raised the switch with his right. . . when suddenly a small miracle occurred; the trance snapped, Peter came unstuck and stampeded off, the descending switch missing him by mere millimetres, his receding rear end galloping away as if twenty wasps had simultaneously stung him there.

Enraged, old Sunflower-Cracker Derksen lumbered off in pursuit, flailing the air, grumbling obscenities and worse. What could be worse, you ask? Well, if you have to ask, you don't know the Mennonite traditions, my friend. You can cheat a Mennonite, you can insult him and you can glance askance at his wife, and all that might be forgiven and often is, but if you propose to question his divine authority in the raising of his children, you are taking your life into your hands. And so it was just as well that Horse-Hiebert was safely in Arkadak and beyond reach of the voice of the old sunflower-cracker, who was shuffling down the road grumping: "Goes courting like a young cock, abandons his farm to a clutch of females, and lets his children run around like rampant cattle! But if I get my hands on that Peter, you mark my words, I'll have him whining and howling like the worst of Hendrik's dogs! He won't be able to sit still for two weeks when I get through with him! Yes, you can count on that!" And he spat the foam from his mouth and said the same things again in Russian, just for good measure, until he had grumbled and groused and spat his way the entire half-mile to the Hiebert farm.

"Hey, in there!" he called to the girls in the kitchen. "Where is the little shit?"

"Not here," said Greta.

"Oho, so they teach you to lie in this place as well! Maybe I'll just have a look-see myself!" And he climbed the stairs to the attic, where, as bad luck would have it, Peter just happened to be. He had fled into the attic and from there into the adjoining hayloft, across a dangerous floor made up of loose boards thrown haphazardly across widely separated joists. He was hunkered down in a far corner, trying to make himself invisible.

The first part of old Sunflower-Cracker Derksen that Peter saw was his unkempt head of hair, rising up through the stair-hatch. Then his cauliflower ears. Then a mouthful of fierce teeth. As he enlarged through the hatch the old man kept calling: "Adam, where are you? Adam, where are you?" And then he caught sight of his quarry in the corner, and his eyes widened triumphantly.

"Yes, yes, just like in Paradise, first disobedient and then trying to hide. But at least Adam only took an apple; this little shit in the corner there, whose pants are shaking with fear, he reached for a stone. Yes yes, but the Good Lord, He always manages to collar these ne'er-do-wells, and so will I. Oh yes, oh yes."

He was coming closer and closer, balancing precariously along the joists, waving his switch menacingly. Peter shrank even farther into the wall. The old man cackled. "And when I've got you, my little Peterkin, I'm going to show you how one tans a stone-thrower's hide like a true professional! I'm going to tan your hide so thoroughly, you'll still be showing the traces two years from now. Oh you just wait and see, you little criminal!"

And suddenly he launched himself forward and made a grab for the trembling boy, but all he got was a fistful of air, because Peter had unwound out of his corner like a released spring and bounded past the old man like a flash, making the boards clatter and heave. And this was something Sunflower-Cracker Derksen had obviously not counted on, because he promptly lost his balance, flailed desperately for surer footing, and fell heavily between two boards, ending up painfully astride one of the underlying joists and wedged in tight. Down below, Peter paused in midflight, saw the old man's predicament, totally forgot himself and called in all the girls. "Hey, come here and have a look at this! Uncle Derksen's pretending to be a cowboy up in the hayloft! But his gelding went and threw him, and now he's riding one of our joists!"

At this the old man became so insanely enraged that steam shot out of his nostrils, and he screamed at Peter: "*Three* weeks, you little criminal! *Three* weeks you won't be able to walk, when I get a hold of you!" which reminded Peter of the problem at hand and he hastily continued his flight down to the nearby creek, where he crawled in among the reeds, the stumps and the dung beetles. And that's where he stayed, hardly daring to breathe more than four or five times a minute, until the sun went down and the milking was done, and everybody calmed down a bit, and even Sunflower-Cracker Derksen Senior had filled his pockets with seeds again, and Willi's head had refilled with the mischief Peter's stone had temporarily knocked out of him.

Finally Peter heard Greta calling: "Peterle, but Peterle, Peterkin, Petrushka, where are you hiding? Come out and come on home! Uncle Derksen went home hours ago and I've been worrying about you; come on out, and I'll even cook you your favourite supper!"

At that Peter raised his head carefully through the bushes, convinced himself of the safety of the situation, promised Him Up There that from that hour on he would scrupulously behave himself, and went with Greta back into the house.

That Monday Horse-Hiebert came home, and during the following week he grew increasingly perplexed at little Peterkin's unusual obedience, industry and tidiness. Finally, on Thursday, still none the wiser, he said to Peter: "Come with me to the barn, my boy; I think we'd better have us a bit of a talk."

And that's what they did. They each sat down on a milkstool in the milking parlour, and it didn't take long for Peter to realize that some bad weather might be brewing, because his father pulled his belt thoughtfully out of his belt loops, doubled it across his knees and demanded: "Now what is it you've got to tell me, hm?"

Now Peter didn't really know what his father might know, but he certainly knew something, that much seemed clear. So he spilled the whole story, all about Sunflower-Cracker Derksen and Willi and the stone, and the chasing and the hayloft and all the rest, telling it all from his own perspective of course, while his father merely nodded thoughtfully without changing his expression.

"Now, would you say that was acceptable behaviour on your part?" Hiebert asked sternly, when the story was over. He was already putting down his pipe.

"Well. . . no," admitted Peter, "but there's something else which I didn't want to tell you, and I didn't. . . see, I really didn't want to say anything about it. . . "

"What's that then," Hiebert demanded shortly, "and make it snappy or I'll polish your rear end even quicker."

At which point the boy played his last trump — laid it, so to speak, down on the milkstool. "Well, I didn't want to tell you this, but do you know what Uncle Derksen said? D'you know what he actually said? He said, 'If that old Horse-Hiebert can't keep his son in check then I'll just have to take over the job myself!'"

"He said *what?!!*" Horse-Hiebert bellowed, springing up and knocking the milkstool flying. "*What* did you say that old rooster-tail said?" And he hurled his belt back through his belt loops and headed off down the road at a dead run. "I'll show that smartmouth whose business it is to raise my children! I'll show that seed-cracker who's boss of my stable! Why that overweening presumptuous interfering cockerel!" And the last our little Peter Peterkin Petrushka saw of his father, he was barging in through the gate of the Derksens' front yard. . .

FERMENTED CRAB-APPLES

(Jegoahrene Tjrebbaupeltjes)

"Children will eat almost anything," Mrs. Preacher Peters assured us, handing my mother a five-gallon pail of dill pickles, or sour cucumbers as we called them.

Well alright, but there are dill pickles and there are dill pickles, and then there are Mrs. Preacher Peters's concoctions. And if you, dear reader, were imagining sealerfuls of delicious little green gherkins floating cheerfully among dill leaves and garlic, you've got another think coming. Mrs. Preacher Peters's dill pickles were long thick yellow monsters, mushy and seedy. "You see, my Abraham can't bite them all that well anymore, and they always give me heartburn, so here you go, Thiessche — something for winter. Besides, children will eat almost anything!"

And then Mrs. Preacher Peters and her Abraham (the old preacher) climbed back onto their democrat, their nag, Barney, gettyupped abruptly as per instructions, and they continued on their way — leaving me to wonder how in heck Mrs. Preacher Peters would know the first thing about what children were prepared to eat — seeing as she had none of her own. "Oh no," I'd once overheard her saying to someone very huffily, "we don't grow the little monsters at our house!"

Mrs. Preacher Peters's history of canning disasters was substantial, and went back at least as far as 1935. That was a bumper year for crab-apples — I remember it very clearly because that's the year I finally got to wear long pants — and the Peters owned over thirty crab-apple trees. That fall they picked crab-apples like nobody's business, and, since they had no kids, the old preacher had to drag them all the way home in big milk pails, his legs buckling and his bones groaning, and his big cap continually slipping down over his eyes.

Once as he was stumbling half-blind down the road he tripped over his mongrel dog, "Go-Lie-Down", and I couldn't help starting to laugh. Preacher Peters pushed his cap laboriously back onto his head and then asked me sourly whether I didn't know that young people didn't laugh at older people. I said no, I didn't know such things. "Well then," he growled, "you get over here and help me put these apples back into the pails — and no dirt or garbage in with them either — or I'll just have to tell your mother where in the Holy Scriptures it says that young louts aren't to laugh at older gentlemans."

Meanwhile Mrs. Preacher Peters had been busy canning crab-apples since sunrise, shoving armful after armful of wood into her big black stove. All day long she rammed crab-apples into glass crocks and sealers, and when the day was finally done, she had more than sixty of them in two long rows on the table, their yellow, red and pink cheeks glowing deliciously in the late-afternoon sun. All that winter the Peters munched preserved crab-apples, almost daily, but on Christmas Day they finally stopped. "Enuff iss enuff!" said Mr. Peters. "Twenty sealers we must keep for next year thrashing time!"

So that's what they did. Spring seeding came and went, the summer crickets chirped, and in July the little swallows left their nests under the barn eaves, but the Peters didn't touch the remaining crab-apples. "For thrashing time, we have to serve something extra-good!" Mrs. Preacher Peters insisted. What she had in mind was cold apple soup, apple preserves, and dark apple cider.

The threshing gang was scheduled to thresh the Peters's place on August 23. Shortly after sunrise the Toews's old John Deere came puttering into the Peters's yard like a giant bush-hen, followed closely by a long row of double grain boxes and hayracks. The fall harvest was underway.

At noon, all the roaring machinery fell silent and the men staggered over to the stock trough to wash up for lunch. The tables were heaped with a magnificent spread, everything a hungry man could desire, but what attracted the most lip-smacking attention was the glorious basinful of preserved crab-apples, waiting to be served for dessert at the end of the table.

But alas — life's joys of anticipation are rarely exceeded by its joys of fulfillment. The apples, it turned out, had spoiled; the whole mess resembled a pile of fermented compost. "Almost like Friesen's Isebrand's homebrew," was Bruno Hamm's tactful assessment.

Now Preacher Peters was almost impossible to embarrass in matters of the pulpit, but when Mrs. Preacher Peters hissed, "You, Abraham, out with that basin, and hurry up about it!" he turned beet-red. He took the unfortunate basin abruptly to the door, flung its contents with an angry heave at the geese who'd come waddling hopefully to his feet, and headed directly for the fields.

The threshing was wrapped up around seven o'clock. After everyone had left, Peters slouched wearily to the barn to milk Long-Legs, Bossy and Blacky. So it wasn't until an hour later that he stumbled — by golly, holy mister and donnerwetter! — across the entire flock of Mrs. Preacher Peters's geese, all twelve of them, lying motionless, stiff and cold by the side of the barn. Mrs. Preacher Peters was absolutely livid. "Holy Moses and by cringlecrackers!! All I can say for you, Abraham, is thank your lucky stars you're a minister, or I'd be squeezing my hands around your skinny neck like a tourniquet, you miserable old sleeping-cap!!"

Preacher Peters reached unconsciously for his cap and adjusted it hastily, scratched his chest and offered meekly: "I'm abysmally sorry, Greta. Can you ever forgive me?" Then he went to the barn and returned with five empty grain sacks. They plucked the geese on the spot, pulled out all their feathers and down, plucked and grumbled and plucked some more, until each sad, limp goose had been stripped to the skin. Then Preacher Peters threw them all in his wheelbarrow and took them to the manure pile. "And I was so looking forward to a fine roast goose for Christmas," Mrs. Peters grumped as they turned out the light. "Now we'll just have to make do with ham."

But that, dear people, wasn't quite the end of the story. Because the next morning when Preacher Peters got up and looked out the front door, there stood the whole army of ridiculously plucked and naked geese, honking and nattering and fussing indignantly. "By golly! just like Adam before his first apple bite," was Preacher Peters's appalled impression. Mrs. Preacher Peters's head swivelled anxiously, hastily checking the yard for nosy neighbours or unexpected passers-by who might be witness to this further shame.

Meanwhile the good Preacher, who'd by now had quite enough, promptly lost his head and attacked his crab-apple orchard with an axe, chopping down every single tree. But when he made for the geese as well, Mrs. Preacher Peters decided that enough was too much. "*Stop!* Abraham, put away that axe. I shall look after this naked congregation myself." So saying, she drove her newly resurrected herd into an empty granary with her broom, where she kept them well hidden and her husband sworn to secrecy until their goosely lives had come to term.

BACON FAT

(Brodfat)

One morning, two weeks before her fiftieth birthday, Mrs. Jake Klassen ignored the alarm and stayed in bed. And when she even failed to show up in the barn for milking, her husband realized something very serious was amiss.

Jake Klassen tried to convince himself that this really meant nothing, that everything would soon settle back into the usual routine. But his hands trembled and his soul clattered restlessly up and down the back stairs of his mind.

When Mrs. Jake Klassen didn't even get up to bake her usual rolls on the following Saturday morning, black spots floated across Jake's vision and he found himself of no further help to himself at all.

And so for the first time in thirty years — and before lunch no less — Jake sat down at his wife Agatha's bedside for a talk.

This is what she said. "I think it's all over with me, Jake. I agree, it does seem awfully soon and unfair. Our youngest is only seven and he won't do too well without me. You'll probably make out all right with the other six — maybe not too well with Mary and Tina, it's true — but otherwise I think you'll manage to make do without me."

And then Agatha said nothing for a good ten minutes, while Jake sat by her bed licking at the bristles of his moustache, trying desperately to keep his fingers from fiddling with everything, and reflecting thoughtfully on this and that. Some of his thoughts made him feel pretty good, others made him feel a bit ashamed, some embarrassed and some even sorry — the way thoughts will when an unseen hand plays the Joker in the card game of Life.

But when Jake Klassen's wife suddenly spoke again, saying "Jake" — actually calling him Jake once more — Klassen couldn't handle it anymore and he said he had to look after the heifers in the barn. He couldn't stand the idea of her watching him wiping away tears.

Fifteen minutes later, when he returned, nothing had changed; he found his wife undeterred from her mournful business. "Yes, it's all over with me, Jake, and I doubt that you'll be able to manage the whole farm by yourself. So here's what I want you to do. After I'm gone, you go over to Mrs. William Martens, you know the one — my second cousin from over in Rosedale; she's been a widow for more than half a year now — you go to see her, and you tell her that you and I have discussed this whole matter between us, and that I'm agreed. She'll be a good mother to our children, and she'll be a good wife to you too."

At that Jake had to leave to look after the heifers again. On his return from the barn he encountered the brightly coloured barnyard rooster, who immediately dug one wing stiffly into the dirt like a rudder and cackled a stern warning: you leave my harem alone, you understand; I'm not kidding around; buzz off! Klassen stared at him in amazement, and at all the things he was suddenly noticing today, things which normally escaped him entirely.

"Boy, anybody who thinks he can predict the future is sure a fool," Jake thought to himself, shaking his head. But he was also thinking — he couldn't help thinking — about Mrs. William Martens. Mrs. William Martens in the kitchen? And in other places too? Would that really work? Some mares really bite and kick when you try to lead them into an unaccustomed barn. "Good God Jake; shame on you!" he reprimanded himself aloud.

On Monday, Klassen took his wife to the clinic and the doctor there looked her over very thoroughly and examined her here and there and everywhere and then he delivered a pitiless verdict: "Cancer absolutely every- where, Mrs. Klassen — our guess is you've got half a year to live. But in case we're wrong we'll prescribe some thorazine for you, and some proxylatolithos too, and we want you to follow a strict diet, be absolutely religious about it now: no pork, nothing fried, no savories and no salt. Can you manage that? Well, goodbye now, and we'll see you next week."

"And you can stuff that where the sun doesn't shine, you medical mister!" Mrs. Klassen muttered under her breath, surprising even herself with her outspokenness, especially considering that she was clearly headed for heaven at an extremely brisk pace.

But that wasn't the only thing that surprised her these days. Because for some weeks, well before she had stopped getting out of bed in the morning, Mrs. Jake Klassen, alias Agatha, had begun to collect all her bacon fat, every splotch and smidgin of it, which she had poured into quart sealers and hidden carefully beneath her bed. Now she counted them daily, all six of them, moving her fingers slowly from one sealed lid to another. "This fat, Mrs. William Martens, you won't get your hands on," she smiled secretly to herself.

Three weeks into her diet, Mrs. Jake Klassen began to see dark blotches before her eyes, and her thoughts began to slip through her fingers like greasy spoons. Her body trembled and shook, and the blood seemed to hesitate in her veins. But when she began to feel the Devil pinching and scratching his way through her innards, her patience snapped. "Enough is enough," she decided, and called little Jakie to her bed. "I can put up with what the Lord has decreed, but the Devil is quite another matter!"

"Go to the kitchen," she instructed Jakie. "And bring me our largest tablespoon."

"You mean without even a bowl?"

"That's right — without."

When Jakie returned with a puzzled face and a spoon, she added: "Now out with you to play with the kittens; I'm tired and I want to sleep." To herself she remonstrated: "You're even starting to fib to your own kids!"

But what had to be had to be. She reached for one of the sealers underneath the bed and prescribed herself two heaping tablespoons of unadulterated bacon fat. "Because what kind of a God would He be if He cared a whit whether I arrived fat as a slaughter-pig or thin as an exclamation mark?" she pointed out to herself. "Besides, if I get much thinner than I am already, He'd never even recognize me." And with that she actually did fall asleep.

So every day, in addition to her medically prescribed diet of porridge with skim milk and no sugar, Mrs. Jake Klassen downed two huge tablespoons of bacon fat.

And what do you think happened? As God is my witness: on Ascension Day, six months after her doctor had foretold her death, Mrs. Jake Klassen got up out of bed and tottered slowly across the yard to the barn. There she informed her amazed husband, "That little matter with Mrs. William Martens? I think you can postpone that a bit. Because next week I'm going to start milking again, and I may even bake Easter bread for Pentecost this year."

When Mrs. Jake Klassen went to see the doctor three weeks later and he looked her over once again from stem to stern, the old medic had to admit it was more than a body could understand. He almost seemed a little irritated about it. But he couldn't deny that the cancer was gone. And Mrs. Klassen wisely refrained from telling him anything about the Devil's pinch.

Teacher Frank Neufeld had been married to Lottie Janzen for about a year. Now the people over there between Rosengard and Burwalde liked Neufeld, not only because he was a good teacher but also because he could coax a good song out of the children — a prized ability when it came to the all-important Christmas Programme. Furthermore, he rarely found it necessary to strap any of his pupils, even though he hailed from Russia.

And his wife? Well, some people felt her name could have been a little less fancy. What was wrong with plain Anna, or Mary, or Nettie? "A name like that is as frivolous and unnecessary as lace on a petticoat," was Mrs. William Toews's opinion.

Well, maybe.

That spring, the spring of 1944, was so wet and muddy, school was closed during Easter for an entire week. All the children waited at home for the sun to dry up the yards and fields and the impassable roads. No one saw the Neufelds for quite a while, and when they even failed to show up for church, Mrs. Rempel announced that she "sensed something". She fetched a large sealer of chicken soup and ordered her oldest son, Hans, to try to deliver it by horse.

It was only two and a half miles to the Neufeld place, but the journey took over an hour. At times Hans' horse barely found footing in the greasy muck. By the time it had ploughed and grunted and panted its way to the Neufeld driveway, it was lathered and trembling with fatigue, and the sealer in Hans' rucksack was churned to a creamy froth.

It was three o'clock in the afternoon, and the Neufelds should have been at home, but their house stood quiet and deserted-looking in the bush. Hans tethered his horse to a tree and knocked on the door. He held his breath, but he heard nothing. He waited, knocked again, but heard only the pounding of his own heart and the faint humming of his head's blood.

He was just about to tuck the sealer between the inside door and the screen when he heard something — a sound from elsewhere, from behind the barn. Hans churned across the yard to investigate. To his astonishment, he found Teacher Neufeld struggling out of the bush, dragging a small oak tree behind him.

But it was the teacher's appearance that startled Hans the most. Dishevelled hair, bedraggled weekday clothes, his face was covered with sweat and he was muddy from top to bottom. Hans rushed over to help. "Good day, can I give you a hand?"

"Good day," Teacher Neufeld said dully, and extended a shaking hand. That's when Hans realized that the sweat on the teacher's face was mainly tears. A teacher, a respected teacher crying his eyes out.

"What in the world has happened?" Hans asked fearfully.

Teacher Neufeld spoke to Hans as if he were an adult. "Last night at ten Lottie began to deliver, and it took so long, so long, it took half the night. Finally around four in the morning little Lottie was born, she was finally born, and she even smiled a little, the little mite, and then she seemed to lose all interest and after a while she closed her eyes, and then she was gone. Simply gone. I tried everything, but nothing helped." And the tears coursed down his muddy cheeks again.

After a while the two of them dragged the tree into the barn. They hauled in two sawbucks and wrestled the tree across them, and then they attacked it with saw and plane. They laboured until sundown, then lit the lamps and continued on until midnight. Every hour or so Teacher Neufeld went inside to look to his slowly recovering wife, and to stoke up the wood stove. When they were finally exhausted, they had a bite to eat and slept a little. At six the next morning they were at it again, and at two that afternoon the little casket was ready. They lined it with woodshavings, and then Teacher Neufeld went inside and came out again with Lottie's bridal dress. He draped this slowly and lovingly over the shavings, making a little bed.

When he went into the house the next time, he returned wearing his Sunday suit and carrying a basket with the tiny Lottie inside. She looked as if she were asleep, so relaxed and so peaceful. He lifted her out gently and kissed her on the forehead, placed her in the little coffin and made her comfortable. Then he nailed the coffin shut. He and Hans carried it out to the stump of the oak from which it had been made, and dug a small grave. Teacher Neufeld began to sing: "Little children, little children, He holds to His breast. . . Like the stars, the heavens, with bright lights adorning. . . They shall shine, like the jewels, bright stars in His crown. . . " and Hans joined in. Then they lowered the coffin into the hole and Teacher Neufeld covered it. . .

The sun had risen again, finally, after all the mud and the rain. It shone brilliantly, almost hurting the eyes. And after a long time the two men turned around and walked silently and sadly into an emptier world.

But from that day on the name Lottie stopped bothering people the way it had before. Some people, in fact, decided that it was a rather fine name to have. Some even said they felt they'd gotten rather fond of it. . .

THE DEVIL ON THE SHIP

(De Schwoata opp'em Schepp)

Peter Reimer's Hans had suddenly grown up. In the spring, when he walked among the young people, he looked a bit like a king's cockerel. When he drew in his jaw a little, the skin below his sideburns actually looked like a set of wattles. When he got angry and his coxcomb reddened and swelled up, he was downright formidable. When he threatened the boys with his peremptory "Do I have to raise my voice about this?!" they scattered in all directions.

So now, in the evenings and on Sundays, Hans wore white socks and glued down his forelock with Brylcreem. He rarely wiped his nose on his sleeve anymore, and certainly never in the company of adults.

Well, it wasn't long before Hiebert's Nettie said "okay", and a wedding was scheduled.

But as the wedding day approached, Reimer's Hans lost more and more of his cockiness. The bald truth of the matter was, the whole prospect had begun to frighten him. But not too much, surely, I hear you say? Well, maybe not, but certainly enough to give him the shakes and quivers. "Mei goodness mie," Mrs. Reimer commiserated. And after watching this for a while, Old Man Reimer said to himself, "We'll just have to do something about this." So on Hans's wedding day, he gave him two doubles, straight up, and then a few more at regular intervals.

It wasn't long before Hans felt so brave, he contemplated wrestling their old bull. He picked up a clod of dirt and flung it happily at the yard rooster, sending him sprawling. He slammed down the chop box lid with such an enthusiastic bang that even Reimer's ancient gelding was startled into kicking at his stall until the shavings flew. And after twisting the sow's tail for good measure, he lurched back across the yard and into the house.

All of which was well and good, but it was clear that such behaviour wasn't going to be appropriate for church, where Nettie was now waiting. Old Man Reimer began to suspect that he might have been a little excessive with his dosages. What seemed called for now was some firm pressure from the opposite direction, and no time to lose. Reimer made for the corner cupboard where the veterinarian supplies were kept, and shook out some handy horse tranquillizers. Hans swallowed them jovially, and off they went! Just to be on the safe side, Old Man Reimer himself drove their new car, and so they all arrived in one piece, figuratively speaking, festooned in their Sunday best.

But now I'm going to have to tell you another piece of bad news. They did, as I said, all arrive in one piece, but in the interim, our Hans had fallen asleep. And try as they might, they couldn't slap or pinch him awake. They jolted him back and forth, they poked his behind, they shouted into his ears. It was all of no use. Hans was and remained on the nod. There stood the bride, decorated and appetizing as a fancy cheesecake; there stood the best men, hair combed and eager as yearlings, and there stood the bridesmaids, laughing nervously to hide the FOR SALE signs on their faces — while the groom simply snored, wheezed and groaned a bit. It was embarrassing beyond description. "Mei mei mei," lamented Mrs. Reimer and twisted her handkerchief into knots.

The guests in the church, meanwhile, sat stolidly and waited. The pianist, Miss Wiens, had already exhausted her repertoire and was taking it again from the top. A few of the more fidgety guests whapped at flies and scratched their heads. As she played, Miss Wiens kept looking over her shoulder so she wouldn't miss the great moment when she was to burst forth with "Here comes the bride! Here comes the bride!" Had she known of the true state of affairs outside, she might have launched into: "Yesterday's Morrow, Brought Us Great Sorrow".

Outside, Old Man Reimer began to take decisive action. Hans was hoisted out of the car and dragged into the church basement. The bride and her entourage followed closely behind, tears trickling down Nettie's cheeks. Old Man Reimer looked so apoplectic that Mrs. Reimer whimpered, "Oh mei oh mei; whatever you do, please please don't start swearing in church!" Once inside, Nettie tried tickling Hans's cheeks, while Old Man Reimer poured a thin stream of water into his nostrils. When Hans's eyes rolled briefly, Reimer made a megaphone of his hands and hollered into his ear: "Hey-ho!! Five o'clock! Time to get up and milk the cows, do the chores, feed the chickens!!" But nothing worked.

Hans slept on.

The whole situation was now so serious that even Preacher Nickel started speaking in Low German.

"Reimer, what is going on here? What have you done with that boy?"

Reimer evaded the question. "Just tell everybody upstairs to give us another five to ten minutes, please!"

After twenty minutes the plans for the church service upstairs had to be abandoned. However, there seemed no good reason to cancel the after-wedding, so everybody moved to the "Lower Auditorium" and began busily feeding on gossip and sandwiches. Once they had gotten used to the idea of a wedding without bride or groom, everything went swimmingly. The mischievous Abraham Reimer, Old Man Reimer's brother, even tried to convince the wedding photographer to take the Old Man's portrait because "His face has so much colour in it; that would go nice with your colour film!" One look at the Old Man's expression, however, convinced the photographer to make himself permanently scarce.

Once everyone had eaten and no one could think of any more reasons to stay, the guests dispersed. When they were gone, the remaining principals held a meeting. Hans had begun to make a few faint noises and had once limply scratched his chest. Maybe he could still be helped to take his Very Important Step. If he could be brought around, and Nettie's entourage was willing. . . They decided not to give up yet.

And sure enough, that evening, after chores, Hans began to show signs of life. The preacher was quickly recalled, Nettie's entourage re-mobilized, and the Reimer's livingroom hastily tidied. When Preacher Nickel arrived, still serious and pale, they were all seated and ready. (The traditional seating arrangements had been slightly adjusted to allow the best man to give the bridegroom a little more than merely moral support.) Then they all sang two verses from "Work For The Night Is Coming, When Man Works No More".

"But for the moment we still can, and must," Preacher Nickel admonished, "even though things were a little nip and tuck today. And you two young ones, you bridal couple, you must always remember to be particularly attentive and vigilant. For married life is like a voyage on a ship. If the ship is commanded by God and the pilot is Jesus Christ, then everything is in good hands. But sometimes the Other One tries to board the ship, that's the devil we call the Black One. And this Black One, he always turns everything into disarray. And today he almost succeeded, didn't he, Hans? Oh yes, my children, we must always stay awake and on our toes! And you two, you Nettie and you Hans, you must send him packing if he ever tries such mischief again, so that he stays off your ship and doesn't lead you off course! Will you promise me that? Yes, well, then everything is okay. And now set sail joyfully and contentedly on the waters of life. And if the Black One ever tries to board your ship again, you Hans, you step on his knuckles with all your weight, so that he slides back down into the depths with a great cry!"

The bride's eyes glistened and she nodded prettily. The bridegroom had to try harder; his eyes still bulged a little. He grunted heavily, pulled himself sluggishly into a straighter sitting position, and lolled his head in a liquid nod. "You. . . you betchurlife," he slurred emphatically, and with feeling. . .

MISTER BRAHMA

(Mistah Brahma)

"If you ever get to Surabaja or Sukabumi in your travels," said Jacob Fehr, who was always interested in a new agricultural proposition, "then take a good look at those Brahma bulls over there. I'm interested in whether the humps on those beasts are just for decoration, or whether they're filled with some sort of porridge or oat silage. And while you're at it, find out if it's true that those Brahma bulls weigh around eighteen hundred pounds sober and a good three thousand pounds when they're mad. Because Enns and the Fast boys were there, and they said something to that effect.

"Oh yes, and they also said those Brahma bulls simply can't stand white people, whether they be *Molotschna* or Old Coloniers or Brethren or Converted, and that if a bleached Mennonite came too close, a genuine Brahma bull would start clawing and lowing, and then blow snot, turpentine and fire out of his funnels.

"Yes indeed," continued Fehr, "I'm told that a bull with such a hump and dirty pants on is as strong as twenty-five *Kanadiers* or thirty Russians, and when he starts firing on all five cylinders he's got about eight to ten horsepower for sale. So you go and find out and report to me. Because Enns and the Fast boys were there and they told me there were twenty times as many of these humpbacks every half mile as in the entire Calgary Stampede."

"Why don't you come along?" I asked him.

"No, I'm too old, and anyway, my arthritis gets me whenever I go up higher than a milking stool, and an airplane goes higher than that, I have that on good authority."

And so I went alone, and I found things in Indonesia just as Fehr had told me: big, stout bulls, a bit phlegmatic, some of them, but very powerful, and they all had humps on their hunchbacks. But when I tried to touch these humps to find out what was in them I found the bulls to be exceedingly opinionated on the subject. Oh yes, exceedingly. I've still got a torn pair of pants to prove it. And as I was standing there looking at my torn pants I remembered an incident from bygone days, when my brother Willie was younger and I was an even nicer guy than I am today.

Willie had read in the *Free Press* that the Royal Fair in Winnipeg was offering three hundred dollars to anyone who could ride their Brahma bull. A very simple affair: you just had to stay on its back for ten seconds, yell "Yippee!" three times and collect your money. Well, three hundred dollars was a lot of money in '51, even in Gruenthal. So we decided to head into Winnipeg to pick up that dough. But first, to be on the safe side, Willie did a little practising at home. He rode all our horses into the ground, broke in a cow and a heifer, and finally even saddled up our stubborn gelding and gave him rein and crop and full speed ahead. Oh yes, you betcha, our Willie was sure a sharpie — sharper than a pocket-knife and almost as sharp as a Gillette.

So off we went to Winnipeg, where sure enough we found the fair, and the horses and the chuckwagons and the bow-legged cowboys, and also that Brahma bull, as big as a camel and twice as mad as Old Man Thiessen fixing fence in mosquito season. Willie sat down on this brute like he was sitting down on lit barbecue coals; fortunately for him it was still in its stall. Then he said he wasn't sitting very comfortable, and couldn't he maybe sit on the tail end and hang on to the hump from behind. But the bull-boys wouldn't go for that. Nothing doing, Willie had to sit between the hump and the hunchback, on the broadest part of the back, with his face aimed into the wind.

So the bull was still in his stall and Willie was trying to make himself a little more at home on its third floor, but when he saw how far down the earth was below him, now that the bull was becoming angrier and more obstreperous, he seemed to be getting a little anxious. And no wonder: the bull-boys had started poking around in the bull's shorts with a cattle prod, giving him enough juice to light up all of Gruenthal and a few toasters and frying pans besides. So the way Willie saw it, it was time to start hedging his bets. "Tell You what, Lord. If I make that three hundred, I'll give half to the mission work and the other half. . ."

"Here comes the *BRAHMA BULL!!*" yelled the rodeo announcer over the loudspeaker, and six thousand people saw Gruenthal's Number One Cowboy rise up on a rocket engine and then start into aerobatic manoeuvers at five hundred feet. "Four seconds and he's still going strong!" the announcer hollered. There were more fiery skytrails and comet tails and then Mr. Brahma seemed to have come to the conclusion that east was east and west was west, but this little freeloader was becoming just a bit too much. He let himself plunge back to earth one last time and then rose straight up like a ton of dynamite going off, with a hula twist at the upper end that snapped him around end for end like a bullwhip. Unfortunately for Willie, he'd forgotten to practise that twist, and when he and the bull landed, they were no longer of one flesh.

The stopwatch had stopped at 4.8 seconds and the bull-boys behind the scenes didn't even want to give Willie a free 7-Up. And boy oh boy, our Willie needed one awfully bad. "Your flying wasn't so bad," father offered when we got him up out of the stock trough. "It's your landings need a little practice. Now wipe off your pants — I hope they only need wiping on the outside — and then let's go home."

SAY THANK YOU, PETER

(Saj Dankscheen, Peta)

George Thiessen in Paraguay was an unusual person, and not merely because he was my uncle. He could cut willow switches with an ordinary pocket-knife and then fashion them into things of wonder. And while he did use them periodically to administer a corrective influence to the backsides of the town's youngsters, he used them mainly to find water. Finally, he could teach any breed or variety of parrot to whistle and sing.

Thiessen hadn't really wanted to go to Paraguay but the Mennonite Central Committee told him to be obedient, that it was God's Will that he go to Paraguay to find water, and last but not least, to curb his parrot's salty tongue a little. And so Thiessen gathered his wife and four children and hied himself to Paraguay, the watermelon cradle of South America.

Thiessen was amazed at what he saw in his new country — monkeys, Indians, naked children and hairy apes. "By gosh and by golly," he was heard to say. He also saw strange birds, gaudy parrots and wild pigs — but only four-legged ones, he was heard to say. "And North Americans with grooved tongues," he noted. "Rascals who only speak one language, and that badly." He decided that they probably hadn't received enough thrashings as children. And that they were even more conceited and stupid than the *Molotschnier* at home.

Finally, when it couldn't be put off any longer, he began digging a hole in the middle of a banana grove for the foundation for a *serrei* or shack. When he wasn't wiping sweat off his brow he hammered in nails, and when he wasn't chasing away monkeys and parrots he retrieved his children, who seemed determined to play with the naked gangs of Indian children. Nevertheless it wasn't long before Thiessen had himself a house, a barn, an outhouse, four piglets, a sow and a parrot twice as big and three times as beautiful as any pigeon cock. "A magnificent whopper!" Thiessen was heard to say. "But talk?" he admitted. "The miserable chicken won't tell you any more than a thirty-year-old deaf and dumb donkey. And if he won't improve his performance I'll cut his tail off right behind the ears!"

"Oh no, oh please no!" his children cried and begged. "Let Peter live, papa! Let our beautiful Peter live, please; we'll have him singing like a wren in no time."

"Okay," Thiessen agreed. "I'll give him another three months. But if he won't talk by then, I'll pull out his feathers one by one."

So the children worked on the uncooperative Peter day and night. Every time they gave him something to eat they all chorused: "Say thank you, Peter, please say thank you!" But Peter merely shook out his feathers, ate twice as much as he deserved and said nothing. He was a cocky one, there was no doubt about it; he roamed and ranged at will, invited himself to the neighbours for free meals, harassed the cats and bit the dogs, molested the monkeys and even dive-bombed the children. But talk?

"Not even a trace," Thiessen noted disgustedly. Sometimes when he was alone with the bird he told him: "You're a smart-ass good for nothing, Peter, you know that! I'll chop your beak off behind the ears, maybe! You're as stupid as the Americans: you just want to eat and meddle, but when it comes to working, you're nowhere to be found. Your job is to learn to talk, you crooked-beaked Ami-pigdog! If you choose to forget that, we'll just have to remedy the situation during my next session with you. . ."

The children kept trying harder, withholding food and sweets in a desperate effort to force Peter to yawp. "Why don't you say thank you, Peter; please please say thank you." But Peter only preened himself, laid a crooked egg and sulked.

It was Saturday evening and the week's work was done. Mrs. Thiessen had baked Mennonite buns, the children had washed their necks and ears, and George Thiessen had even washed his feet for a change. The evening meal was steaming serenely on the table. Suddenly, just as they were saying grace, a terrific uproar erupted among the pigs in the barn. "Tigers, devils, mad apes or Americans among the pigs!" Thiessen hollered and grabbed his shotgun. His eldest, Peter, grabbed an axe and galloped after him, and Mrs. Thiessen grabbed a butcher knife and joined the parade. The pigs were screaming so loudly, you could hardly hear the yells of the Thiessen family army. Within minutes they were lined up and ready at the pigsty gate, their weapons aimed and threatening.

But instead of tigers, devils or mad apes ("Lucky for them it wasn't the Americans!" Thiessen was heard to say), it was Peter, big, bright and cocky Peter, who was bronc-riding a terrorized sow, nipping and snapping her terribly about the ears, and squawking at the top of his lungs: "Say thank you, Peter, say thank you, you lazy devil, you crazy *Molotschnier!* I'll teach you how to talk and right now, too. Say thank you, you pious lazy bastard! I'll chop your tail off right behind your ears, you lazy pigdog you. . ."

SHIT-SCARED

(Shizz)

The leaves of the calendar rolled over in rapid succession, and suddenly it was spring, 1948, with the news that the Red Cross was coming to Gruenthal. It was in the local paper, the school, the church basements and on posters everywhere; they'd be coming in huge trucks filled with five-gallon pails, and what these pails were meant to be filled with was Gruenthaler blood. All able-bodied Mennonites were being urged to donate.

Initial estimates were that about five hundred men and thirty-five women would do so. Then second thoughts caught hold, and within a week those numbers had dwindled by half. By the third week the grand total had shrunk by half again.

When word of this backsliding reached Winnipeg — it was generally suspected that Cafe Driediger's wife had blown the whistle — the Winnipeg Red Cross held an emergency meeting and decided to double the number of doughnuts and remove limits on the amount of Wynola a donor would be permitted to consume in return for his donation. The coffee ration was bumped up to two full cups (or Postum for Mrs. Peter Rempel, whose heart condition was exacerbated by coffee), and all donors' children would receive their fill of sugar cubes. At that the estimates rose sharply once again.

But there were hold-outs. Johan Funk regretted that he probably wouldn't be able to give on the Wednesday in question, because he never washed his arms on Wednesdays. Jacob Toews, who had turned Jehovah's Witness, insisted it was a terrible sin to donate blood. The Old Colony Mennonites announced they wouldn't be donating blood because they were sure that somewhere in the Old Testament such nonsense was expressly forbidden.

My father grumped that he had never really managed to replenish his supply from the time the Reds had shot him through the pants in the year '19. Neudarp's Peter said he would try his best, but that he couldn't guarantee anything; he always tensed up when lying in bed with so many people. And Schuster-Bergen said "No!" and "Notting doing! Sure, I'd like to donate blood, but just have a look at this nose of mine! Do you think anybody would like to get such a schnozz as I have?" And a lot of people agreed that Bergen had a good case, despite the fact that the Red Cross announced that noses were not affected by blood transfusions. "And anyway," Bergen continued, "I always bang my fingers when cobblering, and that is sure to be passed on through the blood!" The Gruenthaler nurse couldn't categorically state otherwise.

Undecided Gruenthalers consulted Peter Klassen for advice. He proved undecided himself. "My wife says I'm such a restless sleeper, I probably couldn't lie still in bed for that long," he sighed. "I'm not at all sure I'd make it."

Cornelius Falk, the stout and stocky member from the Brethren Church, worried that once opened, his veins would gush blood like cow's milk, and there would be no stopping it. "I don't feel it would be in our mutual interest to put the matter to the test," he told the nurses very formally.

Local wizard, Mr. Unger, would have been all for the idea at one time; he was an old hand at giving blood and had done so dozens of times — voluntarily and involuntarily. Oh yes, six times to the Whites in Russia and another thirteen times while a refugee in Germany. But now he'd been in Canada long enough to have lost his familiarity with the sight of blood, and he felt sure he'd faint anytime he saw it. "It's true, I can't even chop a rooster's head off anymore; just ask Mother."

Jacob Klassen stated flatly that all this idiocy just had to be the product of a Communist imagination, and "Who knows what they do with that blood once they've got it? I know for one thing that the Reds always ate a lot of blood sausage in their diet."

Peter Braun felt he had more than filled his quota while in the army. Hans Kaetler refused to put himself into the hands of amateurs who would "poke around with their dull needles and never not locate my veins." And Second-hand Wiens was appalled. "What! Lie down in the middle of the day in bed? What will people think! And anyway, I once did that in Russia shortly after I'd gotten typhoid fever, and what do you think happened? I fell into a coma, that's what. And I certainly don't want that to happen again."

Only Choir Conductor Block smiled quietly and nodded when I told him what I'd heard. "They're scared shitless, Thiessen my lad," he pointed out in a voice as gentle and grave as if he were teaching Sunday school. "They haven't got the nerve of a frozen gopher in March. And now let's get over there and donate some precious bodily fluids, before the *Steinbach Carillon News* finds out about us and gives the Steinbachers the idea they might be good for more than just selling cars!"

MUCH OBLIGED, JAKE!

(Dankscheen, Jasch!)

Jake Neufeld and Peter Braun — or, more accurately (because they were single) Neufeld's Jake and Braun's Peter — were two Mennonite farmers. Well, a little more than just farmers, actually. The two ran a ranch together in southwestern Saskatchewan. Their herd consisted of six hundred cattle and half again as many heifers, and a bunch of beautiful horses.

Life was treating them pretty well. Aside from ranching and making money, their interests consisted mainly of rodeos in the summer and Wilf Carter in the winter. When Wilf Carter was called for, Jake manhandled the gramophone while Peter played accompanying guitar, adding his own lusty yodelling. Often Peter sang and yodelled with so much conviction that the coyotes for miles around aimed their noses at the moon and howled along. People insisted that even the coyotes sobbed when Peter and Wilf sang "My Little Grey-Haired Mother in the West" — though personally, I suspect that's an exaggeration. Not because I have any doubts about the extent to which Peter's beautiful singing and playing could move the heart of any mammal on two or four legs, but simply because coyotes are so busy catching rabbits in the winter, they can't afford to get sentimental. But I have no doubt they appreciated Peter's talents just the same. Coyotes are said to be every bit as musical as the average Mennonite choir director.

Now both these fellows were pleasant enough. Jake was possibly the more miserly of the two, and wasn't above a bit of skullduggery, but Peter was an absolutely straight shooter. Jake's eyes tended to roll a bit more at the sight of a walking pair of pantyhose, while Peter — well, you could see he felt a lot more comfortable on a horse than on a coffee shop chair.

It was early winter in 1951, and the two ranchers had just helped a friend move his cattle to winter range far to the west of their own spread. Returning home, the morning weather had looked promising enough, but by four-thirty that afternoon the sky began to darken and soon after, hard-kernelled flakes began to fly. The temperature plunged sharply.

"So what do you think?" Jake asked Peter. Peter had another slow look around. "No point fighting it," he shrugged. "Looks like winter to me."

"Don't know who lives around here," Jake agreed, "but we'll pull in first chance we get."

They rode for another half-hour. The wind had begun to howl, and the horses' tails and manes flapped wildly in the gusts. It was looking grim. And then, just off to the west, they saw a ranch house and a stable.

When they knocked on the door, the lady who answered seemed apprehensive about taking them in, but when she saw their plight she changed her mind. She let them stable and feed their horses in the barn, then invited them into the house.

During dinner they talked about the weather, about seeding and harvest, about cattle and horses and prospects for the future. It turned out that the lady was a widow; her husband had been bucked off by a bronco in the Great Sandhills and had died shortly thereafter. Her ranch was big and beautiful and she had no intention of leaving it, but it was a struggle to maintain it single-handedly. She had no children, and no close relatives who were interested in ranching.

Before turning in, Peter took down a guitar that was hanging on the diningroom wall, tuned it, and sang a few songs. Outside, the blizzard bucked and bellowed. Inside, the flames in the lamps flickered contentedly. After another hour, the widow showed them to their beds: the window-bench and the sofa. Then she disappeared upstairs.

The next morning the fields around the ranch lay deep in snow as far as the eye could see. But the sky was clear, and the sun rose a brilliant ball on the eastern horizon. Everything sparkled and glittered. The widow was already up, making breakfast. The two men lounged around for another pleasant hour and then took their leave. "That was good," the widow beamed. "The singing, the company. . . everything. Come again anytime."

"We may just do that," they agreed, and turned their horses toward the sun.

The strange thing was, from that day on, Jake and Peter didn't get along as well as they had before. It was nothing in particular, nothing specific, but they found themselves getting on each other's nerves just a little more than usual, and in each other's way as often as not. They did their best not to let this develop unduly, and they tried hard to work around it, but in the end the strain became intolerable, and they decided to call it quits. It was agreed that each would go his own way after the spring seeding.

On April the fifteenth, Peter Braun rode into town for the mail. There was an envelope addressed to him from a law firm in Regina. Inside was a letter from the widow. It read, in part: "I did not tell you when you stayed at my ranch last October that I was terminally ill, because it didn't matter. But you were so loving and gentle with me that night, that I have decided to give you this ranch upon my death. I have no one else who could run it properly, or who would take the kind of care of it that I would want to be assured of. Somehow, I'm convinced that you would." And farther down in the letter: "I have arranged with my lawyers that this letter is not to be forwarded to you until I have passed on. When you receive it, therefore, the ranch will be yours."

Peter just stood there thunderstruck. The letter in his hand shook. He looked utterly perplexed, and just kept shaking his head. Finally he headed slowly for home. And by the time he got there, he'd had enough time to think it all through, and now the questions he needed to ask were at least clear to him. He found Jake pitching the last bales from the stable loft.

"Listen Jake, you remember that night we stayed with that widow on that ranch near Maple Creek? Last October, thereabouts?"

Jake seemed to have no trouble remembering the occasion.

"Okay, now I need a straight answer here. Did you, during that night, I mean after everybody went to bed, you know, did you. . . ah. . . what I'm trying to say is, did you sneak up to that widow's bedroom and. . . ah. . . console her a bit?"

Jake looked faintly apprehensive and seemed to feel that this might not be any of Peter's business. He said as much. But he didn't deny the possibility.

"Well, it just might be more of my business than you think. Because I've got a letter here that. . . ah. . . ah. . . listen Jake, just tell me one more thing, or there's just no way I can really make heads or tails out of this whole thing. . . did you, by any crazy chance, did you tell her your name was Peter, instead of Jake?"

Jake looked like he'd been caught with his fingers in the cookie jar. He hemmed and hawed for a bit, and then he began to stumble his way through an apology.

Peter's face broke into a relieved grin. "No apology necessary, old cock," he assured him. "No damage done. No damage done at all. In fact, you seem to have just given me a ranch. Much obliged, Jake!"

GLOSSARY OF TERMS

Alpenkraeuter
(13)

An alcohol-based herbal tonic.

bonesetter
(64)

A Mennonite version of a chiropractor.

brodfat
(85)

Bacon fat; frying-fat.

Kanadier
(49, 99)

A Mennonite immigrant, usually from the Ukraine-based colonies, who settled in Canada during the 1870s.

kulak
(24)

A rich peasant or peasant-farmer. During the Russian Revolution, the term was applied to most land-owning farmers deemed to have made their money on the backs of the landless class.

kwas
(13)

A sour, mildly alcoholic drink made of black bread, malt and honey.

Molotschna
(12, 99)

A variation on *Molotschnier* (103, 106); someone from the Molotschna, a Mennonite colony in the Ukraine.

Russlaender
(54)

A Mennonite immigrant who came to Canada, usually from the Ukraine-based colonies, in the 1920s.

the Mazursche
(36)

A designation for a female that is patrilineal, similar to the tradition of naming a woman only in connection with her husband, i.e., Mrs. Abraham Schroeder or "the Schroedersche".

Wynola
(107)

A soft drink popular on the Prairies in the 1930s and 1940s.

ABOUT THE AUTHORS

Jack Thiessen is one of a dwindling number of Mennonite Low-German storytellers who are still creating and publishing in this dialect. In addition to his many Low-German stories and poems, published serially in the *Mennonite Mirror* and assembled in such collections as *Predicht fier Haite* (Buske Verlag, Hamburg), he has compiled a Mennonite Low German dictionary (*Mennonitisches Woerterbuch*, Elwert Verlag, Marburg). He is also an English-language novelist (*Faux Pas*, Mosaic Press, Ontario) and essayist. Jack Thiessen recently retired from his position as Professor of German at the University of Winnipeg.

Andreas Schroeder, also an ethnic Mennonite, emigrated to Canada from Germany in 1951. He has made his living for the past 23 years as a poet, novelist, translator, journalist and broadcaster. He has taught Creative Writing and Translation at various universities and colleges, and committed more than his share of cultural politics (Chairman, Writers' Union of Canada; Founding Chairman, Public Lending Right Commission; etc.). His ten books include *Dustship Glory* (documentary novel), *Toccata in 'D'* (novella), *File of Uncertainties* (poetry), *Shaking It Rough* (memoir) and *The Mennonites: A Pictorial History of Their Lives in Canada*.